Apostles of Disunion

Southern Secession Commissioners and the
Causes of the Civil War

A NATION DIVIDED:

STUDIES IN THE CIVIL WAR ERA

Orville Vernon Burton and Elizabeth R. Varon, Editors

APOSTLES *of* DISUNION

*Southern
Secession Commissioners
and the Causes of
the Civil War*

Fifteenth Anniversary Edition

Charles B. Dew

UNIVERSITY OF VIRGINIA PRESS

Charlottesville and London

UNIVERSITY OF VIRGINIA PRESS
© 2001 by the Rector and Visitors of the University of Virginia
Afterword © 2016 by the Rector and Visitors of the University of Virginia
All rights reserved
Printed in the United States of America on acid-free paper

First published 2001
Fifteenth anniversary edition published 2016
ISBN 978-0-8139-3944-5 (paper)

5 7 9 8 6 4

Library of Congress Cataloging-in-Publication Data is available from the
Library of Congress.

For Robb

Contents

Acknowledgments

I am deeply grateful for the help I received on this project. Williams College provided me with much-needed research support and the opportunity to reside at the college's Francis Christopher Oakley Center for the Humanities and Social Sciences. The fellows at the center and my colleagues in the Williams History Department read my work in progress and gave me invaluable advice at critical junctures. I appreciate their criticisms and suggestions more than I can adequately acknowledge here.

I have also benefited from the generosity and expertise of a number of scholars who graciously took time from their own work to look at mine. I wish to thank Robert Dawidoff, Bob Bonner, John Hubbell, Phil Schwarz, Ken Stampp, Jon Wakelyn, Bert Wyatt-Brown, and the late C. Vann Woodward for their criticisms and their encouragement. Jessie Hutcheson deserves my thanks for her help in keeping me updated on Confederate culture in the contemporary South.

I could not have begun to track down the speeches and letters of the secession commissioners without the aid of a great many talented archivists and librarians. My travels took me to a number of institutions, and everywhere I went I invariably received knowledgeable and professional support. I would like to thank the able staff members of the following libraries and archives for all they did for me during my visits: the Library of Congress; the National Archives; the Library of Virginia; the Virginia Historical Society; the Museum of the Confederacy; the University of Virginia Library; the Duke University Library; the University of North Carolina Library; the North Carolina Division of Archives and History; the South Caroliniana Library; the Georgia Department of Archives and History; the Alabama Department of Archives and History; the Montgomery, Alabama, Public Library; the Mississippi Department of Archives and History; the Newberry Library; the Chicago Historical Society; the Minnesota Historical Society; and the State Historical Society of Wisconsin. Special thanks go to the superb staff of the Williams College Library, particularly Lee Dalzell and Alison O'Grady.

Somehow my wonderful typists, GiGi Swift and Brenda Briguglio, managed to turn my handwritten legal sheets into a beautifully typed manuscript. I stand in awe of their skill, not to mention their patience and generosity of spirit.

Dick Holway of the University Press of Virginia went well beyond the normal call of duty in his efforts to support my manuscript. I am deeply grateful for all he has done to bring this book into print.

Finally, I wish to thank Robb Forman Dew for her tireless help and support. Without her presence in my life, this project would never have seen the light of day. Her name on the dedication page is grossly inadequate thanks for all she has done to sustain my efforts, here and at countless other times.

Apostles of Disunion

Southern Secession Commissioners and the
Causes of the Civil War

Introduction

ALTHOUGH I have taught at a New England college for the past twenty-three years, I am a son of the South. My ancestors on both sides fought for the Confederacy, and my father was named Jack, not John, because of his father's reverence for Stonewall Jackson. On my fourteenth birthday I was given a .22-caliber rifle and Douglas Southall Freeman's *Lee's Lieutenants*. I devoured all three volumes of Freeman's classic history of the Army of Northern Virginia, and the rifle was my constant companion during those seemingly endless summer days in Florida when plinking at cans and dreaming of Civil War battles constituted a significant part of my boyhood activities. When I went off to high school in Virginia, I packed a Confederate battle flag in my suitcase and hung it proudly in my dorm room. My grandmother, whom I loved dearly, was a card-carrying member of the United Daughters of the Confederacy.

I did not think much about secession and the causes of the war back then. My focus was on the battlefield and Lee's valiant men, who had fought so hard and so long before finally yielding to overwhelming numbers. But if anyone asked me what the war was all about, I had a ready answer for them. I knew from listening to adult conversations about The War, as it was called, and from my limited reading on the subject that the South had seceded for one reason and one reason only: states' rights. As I recall, my principal written source for this view was a small paperback entitled *A Confederate Youth's Primer,* a gift from one of my father's law partners. It was crystal clear to me that the Southern states had left the Union to defend their just and sovereign rights—rights the North was determined to deny my region and my ancestors. Anyone who thought differently was either deranged or a Yankee, and neither class deserved to be taken seriously on this subject.

All this is a roundabout introduction to a point I wish to make at the outset: despite my scholarly training and years spent trying to practice the historian's craft, I found this in many ways a difficult and painful book to write. Even though I am far removed—both in time and attitude—from my boyhood dreaming about Confederate glory, I am still hit with a profound sadness when I read over the material on which this study is based.

I vividly recall the first time I encountered the secession commissioners' words. I was not long out of graduate school and was combing through volume 1 of series 4 of the *Official Records of the Union and Confederate Armies*—the series dealing with the Southern home front—looking for material on wartime manufacturing. For some reason Stephen F. Hale's letter to the governor of Kentucky—the document that constitutes the core of chapter 4 of this book—caught my eye, and I read the letter through from start to finish. I was stunned by what I found there. Hale's rhetoric took me back in an instant to my childhood growing up in the South on the white side of the color line. There, in this December 1860 document, were the same sentiments, the same views, indeed even some of the same ugly words, that I had heard used to justify racial segregation during my own youth. Could secession and racism be so intimately connected, I asked myself? I knew, of course, that the institution of slavery was on the line in 1860–61, but did white supremacy also form a critical element in the secessionist cause, a cause my ancestors fought for and that my relatives revered? The present volume—an examination of the message the secession commissioners carried across the South in late 1860 and early 1861—attempts to answer these questions.

Like any student of secession, I know that I have not presented the whole story here. The scholarship on this topic is rich and varied and points to a multitude of causal factors. A number of seminal studies—particularly books by Michael F. Holt, J. Mills Thornton III, and Daniel W. Crofts and an insightful article by Peyton McCrary, Clark Miller, and Dale Baum—have taken us deep into the political world of the late antebellum South and shown us how complex the relationship was between slavery, the Southern electorate, and the decision for secession in 1860–61.[1] Other scholars, most notably Bertram Wyatt-Brown and Kenneth S. Greenberg, have pointed to cultural factors—notions of honor and ideas about coercion, tyranny, and republicanism—that colored the way Southerners reacted to what they saw as Northern moves against Southern interests in the years leading up to the war.[2]

I have no quarrel with any of these historians, and I have learned a great deal from their work. But I am convinced that the speeches and letters of the Southern commissioners of 1860–61 also reveal a great deal about secession and the coming of the Civil War. I believe deeply that the story these documents tell is one that all of us, northerners and southerners, black and white, need to confront as we try to understand our past and move toward a future in which a fuller commitment to decency and racial justice will be part of our shared experience.

CHAPTER I

Slavery, States' Rights, and Secession Commissioners

(("T HE Civil War was fought over what important issue?" So reads one of twenty questions on an exam administered by the Immigration and Naturalization Service to prospective American citizens. According to the INS, you are correct if you offer either one of the following answers: "Slavery or states rights."[1]

It is reassuring to know that the INS has a flexible approach to one of the critical questions in American history, but one might ask how the single "issue" raised in the question can have an either/or answer in this instance—the only time such an option occurs on the test. Beyond that, some might want to know whether "slavery" or "states rights" is the more correct answer. But it is probably unfair to chide the test preparers at the INS for trying to fudge the issue. Their uncertainty reflects the deep division and profound ambivalence in contemporary American culture over the origins of the Civil War. One hundred and forty years after the beginning of that fratricidal conflict, neither the public nor the scholarly community has reached anything approaching a consensus as to what caused the bloodiest four years in this country's history.

There is no doubt whatsoever about the sequence of events that triggered the outbreak of hostilities in the spring of 1861. In the wake of Abraham Lincoln's triumph at the polls in the presidential election of 1860, seven states of the lower South—South Carolina, Mississippi, Florida, Alabama, Georgia, Louisiana, and Texas—seceded from the Union. Beginning with South Carolina on December 20, 1860, and ending with Texas on February 1, 1861, secession conventions in these seven states passed ordinances severing all ties to the national government. A convention meeting in Montgomery, Alabama, in early February 1861 drafted a constitution for the Confederate States of America and organized a provisional government that rushed military forces into the field.

The flashpoint came in Charleston, South Carolina. Early in the morning on April 12, 1861, Confederate shore batteries opened fire on the Union garrison occupying Fort Sumter in Charleston harbor. In the aftermath of the Sumter bombardment and Lincoln's call for volunteers to suppress the rebellion, four additional slave states—Virginia, North Carolina, Tennessee, and Arkansas—joined the original seven, and the war was on.

The question about which so much controversy has swirled is the obvious one: what caused the seven Deep South states to secede? Why did the election of a Republican president in November 1860 trigger such a swift, revolutionary, and potentially dangerous response? If we can get inside the secessionist mind-set, if we can understand what was driving the lower South in the great secession winter of 1860–61, we can go a long way toward explaining the coming of the American Civil War.

Civil War causation is certainly not an arcane subject for many Americans, as newspapers, magazines, and other media outlets remind us on an almost daily basis.

On July 27, 1999, the *Richmond Times-Dispatch* bore the headline "Council Supports Mural of Lee" across the full width of its front page. The night before, the Richmond City Council had engaged in a contentious debate over whether or not a portrait of Robert E. Lee should be included in an outdoor display at the newly developed Canal Walk along the James River. The vote, six to three in favor of hanging a larger-than-life-sized picture of Lee as part of a floodwall gallery, came after hours of public comment by individuals passionately in favor of, or opposed to, Lee's inclusion.

The council's decision was, presumably, the final act in a dispute that had produced heated exchanges in the city for over a year. During that time the state and local chapters of the National Association for the Advancement of Colored People had come out strongly against the Lee portrait, and one city councilman had described the Confederate general as "akin to Adolf Hitler" and insisted that "Lee should not be honored in public because he supported slavery by fighting for the Confederacy." Pro-Lee advocates included the Sons of Confederate Veterans organization, which mounted a rally on the grounds of the Virginia State Capitol, and former Ku Klux Klan leader David Duke, who graced the city with his presence less than a fortnight before the council voted in favor of Lee's presence on the concrete floodwall.[2]

The fight over the Lee portrait was only the latest in a string of controversies in Virginia that has focused public attention on the state's Confederate past. In 1998 Virginians carried out a spirited debate over the merits of Republican governor James S. Gilmore's proclamation naming April "Confederate History Month" in the Old Dominion. Gilmore's official message referred to the Civil War as "a four-year tragic, heroic and determined struggle for deeply held beliefs," although the governor made no attempt to spell out exactly what those beliefs might be. Gilmore then went on to say something about slavery (a subject his Republican predecessor, Governor George Allen, had studiously avoided in his earlier, equally controversial Confederate History Month proclamations). "Slavery was a practice that deprived African-Americans of their God-given inalienable rights [and] which degraded the human spirit," Gilmore said.[3]

The governor's attempt to work both sides of the street failed miserably. The Virginia NAACP Conference deplored the celebration of Confederate History Month once again in the state, although the conference commended the governor for "being inclusive and respecting the horrors of African enslavement." But R. Wayne Byrd Sr., the president of the Virginia Heritage Preservation Association, had a much different reaction to the governor's statement; he saw the proclamation as nothing less than "an insult" to white Virginians. Byrd, appearing at a news conference at the State Capitol with a small Confederate flag pinned to his lapel, "went on to say he had 'a problem' with Gilmore calling slavery a cause of the Civil War and 'an abhorred' practice." According to press reports, Byrd was accompanied at this Richmond news conference by "a half-dozen other business-suited Confederate enthusiasts, including former Virginia GOP Chairman Patrick S. McSweeney."[4]

The past, it seems fair to say, is far from dead in the southern reaches of the United States. The Virginia fights over the Lee portrait and Confederate History Month are only two of many debates roiling the contemporary South over the respect, or disrespect, that should be afforded the Lost Cause. Certainly the most prominent recent controversy has been the fight over whether or not the Confederate battle flag should float over the South Carolina State Capitol.

In January 2000 demonstrators both for and against flying the flag descended on Columbia. A proflag group of some 6,000 supporters who gathered on January 8 was followed nine days later by close to 50,000 antiflag marchers who constituted what may well have been the largest civil rights demonstration in the South since the 1960s. The smaller numbers favoring the flag, many of whom were clad in

Confederate uniforms, defended the "Stars and Bars" as "a symbol of Southern heritage" and "a reminder of their ancestors' courage in battling to secede from the Union."[5] Many of the antiflag demonstrators carried placards reading "Your Heritage Is My Slavery," and speaker after speaker denounced the flag "as a symbol of slavery and hatred."[6] The National Association for the Advancement of Colored People had earlier called for an economic boycott of South Carolina until the flag was removed from its place of honor above the Capitol dome.[7]

The pressure for a boycott exerted by a national civil rights organization obviously hit a raw nerve in the state. Nowhere was this more evident than at the January 8 rally of flag supporters in Columbia. A South Carolina state senator addressing the crowd hurled defiance at the NAACP. "Can you believe that there are those who think the General Assembly of South Carolina is going to . . . knuckle under" to "that organization known as the National Association for Retarded People?" asked Senator Arthur Ravenel, Republican from Mount Pleasant.[8] When asked for his reaction to Senator Ravenel's statement, Lonnie Randolph, a leader of the NAACP boycott, replied, "We don't dignify ignorant comments and ignorant statements with a response."[9] Senator Ravenel subsequently apologized to "retarded people" for linking them to the NAACP.[10]

Virginia and South Carolina are hardly the only places where Confederate symbols have stirred controversy. If things keep going the way they have in recent years, acrimonious historical debate may soon rival kudzu for prominence on the southern landscape.

Tempers flared in Maryland after the Motor Vehicle Administration issued a vanity license plate for the Sons of Confederate Veterans bearing a small Confederate flag. "Maryland doesn't need to go backwards with this Jim Crow mess," observed the leader of the state's Legislative Black Caucus. A Maryland member of the Sons of

Confederate Veterans insisted that the plates were nothing more than "a symbol of pride in our heritage."[11]

In 1997, as part of a campaign to gain greater national recognition for his school and to improve its image, Chancellor Robert C. Khayat of the University of Mississippi at Oxford asked Ole Miss students and alumni to give up the time-honored tradition of waving the Confederate flag at university sporting events. An Ole Miss faculty member supporting the chancellor called the Rebel flag "the most inflammatory symbol that the South has," but a prominent alumnus saw nothing wrong with the practice. Filling the stands with flag-wavers "makes this place truly unique," he said, and he added, "We don't need the nation's blessing."[12]

Georgians may not be far away from a renewed battle over their state flag. The Georgia chapter of the Reverend Jesse Jackson's Rainbow/PUSH organization may call for a boycott of that state because the Georgia banner incorporates the red, white, and blue Saint Andrew's cross of the Confederate battle flag.[13] Georgia governor Zell Miller had earlier given up his fight to remove this symbol from the state's flag as a lost cause.[14]

This listing could go on and on, but perhaps it will do to mention two additional Confederate straws in the wind of contemporary American culture.

Mississippi, a glossy magazine obviously aimed at an up-scale readership, refers to the Civil War as "The War of Northern Aggression."[15]

The League of the South, an organization founded in Alabama in 1994, aims to further the cause of "secession and Southern independence." The league claims to have chapters in twenty-seven states and boasts a membership numbering in the thousands, including tenured faculty members at institutions like Emory University, the University of South Carolina, and Texas Christian University. League president

Michael Hill insists that "the day of apologizing for the conduct of our Confederate ancestors is over." [16]

And so it goes. Neo-Confederate web sites, bumper stickers, and T-shirts proliferate, and national journalists turn to this rising tide of pro-Dixie sentiment as a subject worthy of book-length investigation.[17] Little wonder, then, that the Immigration and Naturalization Service provides two correct answers to its question on Civil War causation.

Historians seem no more able to agree on the causes of the war than the public at large. Indeed the slavery versus states' rights argument is only the tip of a very large scholarly iceberg. Differing ideologies, separate cultures (and cultural origins), clashing economies, blundering and/or paranoid leaders, failed political parties, conflicting notions of honor, antagonistic political philosophies, the rivalry between a modernizing, bourgeois, free-labor North and a prebourgeois, planter-dominated, slave-labor South—all these and more have been offered up by recent students of this era as the primary reasons behind Southern secession.[18]

Despite this multitude of scholarly voices, however, almost all historians recognize the central role that the institution of slavery and the concept of states' rights played in fostering disunionist sentiment in the Deep South.[19] There is simply no way to avoid these two factors, in part because the secession conventions and Southern political leaders referred to them constantly in their efforts to explain why their states were leaving the Union.

The secessionists of 1860–61 certainly talked much more openly about slavery than present-day neo-Confederates seem willing to do. There are clear, unambiguous references to slavery in many of the official documents that emerged from the secession conventions of the lower South. A defense of states' rights is also there, to be sure, but no attempt was made to hide concern over the fate of the South's slave system in a United States ruled by a Republican majority.

Two states attached preambles to their secession ordinances that reflect this anxiety over the future of slavery. The language was more guarded here than in other areas of the conventions' proceedings, but the meaning was unmistakable. The Alabama preamble charged that the party of Lincoln was "avowedly hostile to the domestic institutions and to the peace and security of the people of the State of Alabama" and indicted the North for "many and dangerous infractions of the Constitution of the United States." [20] In like manner the Texas ordinance berated the national government for its failure "to accomplish the purposes of the compact of union between these States in giving protection either to the persons of our people upon an exposed frontier or to the property of our citizens." The Texas preamble went on to say that under a Lincoln administration, "the power of the Federal Government is . . . to be made a weapon with which to strike down the interests and prosperity of the Southern people, instead of permitting it to be as it was intended—our shield against outrage and aggression." [21]

The Texas delegates gave much fuller voice to their apprehensions in a "declaration of causes" passed the day after the secession ordinance. With Lincoln's election the country had fallen under the control of "a great sectional party . . . proclaiming the debasing doctrine of the equality of all men, irrespective of race and color—a doctrine at war with nature, in opposition to the experience of mankind, and in violation of the plainest revelations of Divine Law," the Texans charged. Republicans could now press forward with their nefarious agenda: "the abolition of negro slavery" and "the recognition of political equality between the white and negro races." [22]

The South Carolina, Georgia, and Mississippi conventions

expressed similar concerns in official declarations setting forth their reasons for leaving the Union.

South Carolina's "Declaration of the Immediate Causes Which Induce and Justify Secession" included a list of long-standing constitutional violations by the free states, but it focused primarily on the Northern embrace of antislavery principles and the evil designs of the newly triumphant Republican Party. The states of the North "have encouraged and assisted thousands of our slaves to leave their homes; and those who remain, have been incited by emissaries, books and pictures to servile insurrection," the South Carolinians claimed. With Lincoln's inauguration on March 4, "this party will take possession of the government . . . , the South shall be excluded from the common territory . . . , and a war must be waged against slavery until it shall cease throughout the United States." [23]

The Georgia Convention was equally outspoken on the subject of slavery. "For twenty years past, the Abolitionists and their allies in the Northern states, have been engaged in constant efforts to subvert our institutions, and to excite insurrection and servile war among us," wrote Robert Toombs, the author of Georgia's declaration of causes. Constitutional protections would become nothing but "parchment rights" in the "treacherous hands" of Republican rulers, whose "avowed purpose is to subject our society, and subject us, not only to the loss of our property but the destruction of ourselves, our wives and our children, and the desolation of our homes, our altars, and our firesides." [24]

The ideas in Mississippi's official statement closely paralleled those of the South Carolina and Georgia pronouncements. "Our position is thoroughly identified with the institution of slavery," Mississippi's "Declaration of Immediate Causes" freely acknowledged. "There was no choice left us but submission to the mandates of abolition, or a dissolution of the union, whose principles had been subverted to work our ruin." The Mississippi document, after citing a number of hostile acts against slavery going back to the Northwest Ordinance of 1787, charged that a Northern abolitionist majority now "advocates negro equality, socially and politically, and promotes insurrection and incendiarism in our midst." Under these circumstances there was only one choice left for their state. "Utter subjugation awaits us in the Union, if we should consent longer to remain in it," the declaration concluded. "We must either submit to degradation and to the loss of property worth four billions of money, or we must secede from the Union."[25]

No such language appeared in Jefferson Davis's inaugural address, however. His first speech as president of the Confederate States of America, delivered in Montgomery on February 18, 1861, was, and remains, a classic articulation of the Southern position that resistance to Northern tyranny and a defense of states' rights were the sole reasons for secession. Constitutional differences alone lay at the heart of the sectional controversy, he insisted. "Our present condition . . . illustrates the American idea that governments rest upon the consent of the governed, and that it is the right of the people to alter or abolish governments whenever they become destructive of the ends for which they were established." The Federal Constitution "had been perverted from the purposes for which it was established," Davis claimed. As a consequence, the seceding states had decided that "the government created by that compact should cease to exist." In abandoning the Union, these states had "merely asserted a right which the Declaration of Independence of 1776 had defined as inalienable," he went on. The South was doing nothing revolutionary; the time had simply arrived when it was necessary for Southerners "to preserve our own rights and promote our own welfare." Nowhere in his address did Davis mention the institution of slavery.[26]

But just over a month after Davis spoke, his vice president, Alexander H. Stephens of Georgia, provided a striking counterpoint to Davis's inaugural address. Fresh from the Constitutional Convention at Montgomery, Stephens told a large and enthusiastic crowd in Savannah on March 21 that the South's "new Constitution has put at rest *forever* all the agitating questions relating to . . . the proper status of the negro in our form of civilization." Thomas Jefferson and the Founding Fathers had believed "that the enslavement of the African was in violation of the laws of nature; that it was wrong in principle, socially, morally, and politically," Stephens said. "Those ideas, however, were fundamentally wrong. They rested upon the assumption of the equality of races. This was an error," he continued. "Our new Government is founded upon exactly the opposite idea; its foundations are laid, its cornerstone rests, upon the great truth that the negro is not equal to the white man; that slavery, subordination to the superior race, is his natural and moral condition." The Confederacy was thus "the first Government ever instituted upon principles in strict conformity to nature and the ordination of Providence, in furnishing the materials of human society." [27]

According to one biographer of Jefferson Davis, the Confederate president "was dismayed at the lack of political tact exhibited by his Vice-President" in this "rabble-rousing address at Savannah." [28] Yet just a few weeks after Stephens spoke, Davis himself interjected the slavery issue into a major speech reviewing the causes of the war. The Northern majority in Congress had engaged in "a persistent and organized system of hostile measures against the rights of the owners of slaves in the Southern States," Davis told the Confederate Congress on April 29, 1861. "Fanatical organizations . . . were assiduously engaged in exciting amongst the slaves a spirit of discontent and revolt; means were furnished for their escape from their owners; and agents secretly employed to entice them to abscond," he insisted. The Republican Party, gripped by "a spirit of ultra fanaticism," was determined to deny slave owners access to the territories and would surround the South with "states in which slavery should be prohibited . . . thus rendering property in slaves so insecure as to be comparatively worthless." Davis described slavery itself as an institution which "a superior race" had used to transform "brutal savages into docile, intelligent, and civilized agricultural laborers," now numbering close to 4 million chattel in the South. "With interests of such overwhelming magnitude imperiled, the people of the Southern States were driven by the conduct of the North to the adoption of some course of action to avert the danger with which they were openly menaced," Davis concluded.[29]

Such frank discussion of the slavery issue disappeared once the war was over, however. Writing from the ashes of Confederate defeat, both Davis and Stephens reverted to a passionate insistence that states' rights, and states' rights alone, lay at the root of the recent conflict. Their postwar apologias offer scarcely a clue that anything other than the defense of constitutional principle was responsible for launching the South on the tides of war.

From his Fort Warren prison cell in Boston harbor in the summer of 1865, Stephens claimed he had been misquoted in his now infamous 1861 "Cornerstone" speech. "The reporter's notes, which were very imperfect, were hastily corrected by me," Stephens insisted, "and were published without further revision and with several glaring errors." What he had meant to say, Stephens went on, was that "slavery was without doubt the occasion of secession," but only because Northern states had ignored their "constitutional obligation as to rendition of fugitives from service, a course betraying total disregard for all constitutional barriers and guarantees." The unfortunate "cornerstone" metaphor had been used "merely to illustrate the firm conviction of the framers of the new [Confederate] Constitution that this relation of the black to white races, which existed in 1787, was not wrong in itself, either morally or politically," and that the institution of slavery "was in conformity to nature and the best for both races." Thus the Confederate Constitution had left the "status of the African race . . . just where it was in the old; I affirmed and meant to affirm nothing else in this Savannah speech."[30]

If the Savannah reporter had misquoted Stephens, so had an Atlanta journalist just eight days earlier. On March 13, 1861, the *Atlanta Southern Confederacy* carried a lengthy report on a speech Stephens had delivered in that city the previous evening. The climax of the vice president's address came when he affirmed that the framers of the Confederate Constitution had "solemnly discarded the pestilent heresy of fancy politicians, that all men, of all races, were equal, and we had made African *inequality* and subordination, and the *equality* of white men, the chief corner stone of the Southern Republic." Stephens made no reference to his Atlanta remarks in his Fort Warren diary.

The former vice president of the Confederacy developed his postwar explanation for the coming of the conflict at much greater length, and with much more florid language, in his *A Constitutional View of the Late War between the States,* the first volume of which appeared in 1868. The war "had its origin in *opposing principles,*" Stephens insisted. "It was a strife between the principles of Federation, on the one side, and Centralism, or Consolidation, on the other." The institution of slavery "was but *the question* on which these antagonistic principles . . . were finally brought into actual and active collision with each other on the field of battle." There could be "no greater violence . . . done to the truth of History" than to refer to the Southern opponents of Northern "Consolidationists" as a "Pro-Slavery Party." The American Civil War, Stephens concluded, represented a struggle between "the friends of Constitutional Liberty" and "the Demon of Centralism, Absolutism, [and] Despotism!"[31]

Jefferson Davis used much more measured language in his *The Rise and Fall of the Confederate Government,* published in 1881, but his analysis of Civil War causation closely paralleled that of his former vice president. "To preserve a sectional equilibrium and to maintain the equality of the States was the effort on one side," he wrote; "to acquire empire was the manifest purpose of the other." The "sectional hostility" that developed before 1861 "was not the consequence of any difference on the abstract question of slavery," Davis claimed. "It would have manifested itself just as certainly if slavery had existed in all the States, or if there had not been a negro in America." Nothing less than "the systematic and persistent struggle to deprive the Southern States of equality in the Union" had led first to mounting political antagonism and then finally to war. "The truth remains intact and incontrovertible, that the existence of African servitude was in no wise the cause of the conflict, but only an incident," he argued; "to whatever extent the question of slavery may have served as an *occasion,* it was far from being the *cause*." The South had fought for the noblest of principles, Davis concluded: for "constitutional government," for "the supremacy of law," and for "the natural rights of man." [32]

So where does all this backing and filling leave us in our efforts to understand why the war came? Unlike present-day South Africa, the nineteenth-century South saw no Truth and Reconciliation Commission established at the end of the Civil War to investigate the causes of that bloody conflict. We Southerners thus did not have to come to grips with our own history at a time when honesty might have carried the day. What we got was the insistence of men like Stephens, Davis, and other former Confederates that slavery had absolutely nothing to do with the South's drive for independence, a claim picked up and advocated by neo-Confederate writers and partisans of the present day. [33]

There is, however, a remarkably clear window into the secessionist mind that has been largely ignored by students of this era. If we want to know what role slavery may or may not have played in the coming of the Civil War, there is no better place to look than in the speeches and letters of the men who served their states as secession commissioners on the eve of the conflict.

As sectional tension mounted in late 1860 and early 1861, five states of the lower South—Mississippi, Alabama, South Carolina, Georgia, and Louisiana—appointed commissioners to other slave states and instructed them to spread the secessionist message across the entire region. These commissioners often explained in detail why their states were exiting the Union, and they did everything in their power to persuade laggard slave states to join the secessionist cause. From December 1860 to April 1861, they carried the gospel of disunion to the far corners of the South.

The overwhelming majority of the commissioners came from the four Deep South states of Mississippi, Alabama, South Carolina, and Georgia. In Mississippi and Alabama the commissioners were appointed by the governor and thus took the field first. In South Carolina, Georgia, and Louisiana, the secession conventions chose the commissioners.

The number of men sent on this vital mission varied from state to state. Mississippi and Alabama named commissioners to every one of the fourteen other slave states. South Carolina, however, only appointed commissioners to those states which had announced they were calling secession conventions, so only nine representatives eventually went out from the cradle of the secession movement—to Alabama, Mississippi, Georgia, Florida, Louisiana, Texas, Arkansas, Virginia, and North Carolina. Georgia dispatched commissioners to six of these same states—Alabama, Louisiana, Texas, Arkansas, North Carolina, and Virginia—and added the border slave states of Maryland, Delaware, Kentucky, and Missouri to the list. The Louisiana Convention appointed a single commissioner, to neighboring Texas, and he did not arrive in Austin until well after the Texas Convention had passed its ordinance of secession.

In all, some fifty-two men served as secession commissioners in the critical weeks just before the Civil War. These individuals were not, by and large, the famous names of antebellum Southern politics. They were often relatively obscure figures—judges, lawyers, doctors, newspaper editors, planters, and farmers—who had had modest political careers but who possessed a reputation for oratory. Sometimes they were better known—ex-governors or state attorneys general or members of Congress. Often they had been born in the states to which they were sent; place of birth was clearly an important factor in the choice of a number of commissioners.

The commissioners appeared in a host of different venues. They addressed state legislatures, they spoke before state conventions called to consider the question of secession, they took the platform before crowds in meeting halls and in the streets, and they wrote letters to governors whose legislatures were not in session. To a man, what they had to say was, and remains, exceedingly instructive and highly illuminating.

Despite their enormous value, the commissioners' speeches and letters have been almost completely overlooked by historians and, as a consequence, by the public at large.[34] This scholarly neglect is difficult to understand. Contemporaries in both North and South paid close attention to the commissioners' movements and what they had to say. Many of their speeches were reprinted in full in newspapers and official state publications, and several appeared in pamphlet form and apparently gained wide circulation.[35] Accounts of the secession crisis published during and just after the war also devoted considerable space to their activities.[36] In the late nineteenth century when

editors at the War Department were assembling a documentary record of the Civil War, they included extensive coverage of the commissioners in the volume dealing with the onset of the conflict—a
clear indication that they considered these men to be key players in
the sequence of events leading up to the war.[37]

Dwight Lowell Dumond highlighted the importance of the commissioners in his 1931 study of the secession movement, a book that
remains the most detailed scholarly treatment of this subject. He described the commissioners' words as extraordinarily important and
revealing. "From the speeches and writings of the commissioners,
as nowhere else, one may realize the depth of feeling and the lack
of sympathy between the two sections of the country," Dumond
wrote. "Vividly denunciatory of a party pledged to the destruction
of Southern institutions, almost tragic in their prophetic tone, and
pleading for a unity of allied interests, they constitute one of the
most interesting series of documents in American history," he went
on to say.[38]

Yet Professor Dumond's book provides little detailed coverage of
what these men actually said, and that pattern has persisted in the
torrent of literature on the Civil War that has appeared in subsequent
decades. As Jon L. Wakelyn notes in his recent *Southern Pamphlets on
Secession*, "No adequate study of the Lower South delegates sent
to the Upper South exists," and that same observation could be
made about the commissioners who addressed their remarks to fellow
Southerners in the states of the Deep South as well.[39] Indeed, Professor Wakelyn does not include the full text of a single commissioner's
speech in his otherwise superb collection of pamphlet literature, even
though, in my opinion, several of the addresses published in pamphlet
form are among the most powerful and revealing expressions of the
secessionist persuasion put to paper on the eve of the war.

I have managed to locate the full texts or detailed synopses of forty-one of the commissioners' speeches and public letters. It is, as Professor Dumond suggested, a truly remarkable set of documents. What is most striking about them is their amazing openness and frankness. The commissioners' words convey an unmistakable impression of candor, of white Southerners talking to fellow Southerners with no need to hold back out of deference to outside sensibilities. These men infused their speeches and letters with emotion, with passion, and with a powerful "Let's cut to the chase" analysis that reveals, better than any other sources I know, what was really driving the Deep South states toward disunion.

The explanations the commissioners offered and the arguments the commissioners made, in short, provide us with extraordinary insight into the secession of the lower South in 1860–61. And by helping us to understand the "why" of secession, these apostles of disunion have gone a long way toward answering that all-important question, "The Civil War was fought over what important issue?"

CHAPTER 2

The First Wave

"IT would be as reasonable to expect the steamship to make a successful voyage across the Atlantic with crazy men for engineers, as to hope for a prosperous future for the South under Black Republican rule." This was the message that Governor John J. Pettus of Mississippi delivered to his state legislature on November 26, 1860, less than three weeks after Abraham Lincoln's election as the sixteenth president of the United States. "Can the lives, liberty and property of the people of Mississippi be safely entrusted to the keeping of that sectional minority which must hereafter administer the Federal Government?" Pettus asked. "Our deliverance from this great danger, in my opinion, is to be found in the reserved right of the States to withdraw from injury and oppression," the governor went on. Secession was the only way to avoid the blight of "Black Republican politics and free negro morals"—forces that would transform Mississippi, in the governor's estimation, into "a cess pool of vice, crime and infamy." [1]

Immediate steps needed to be taken. The legislature should authorize a state convention to consider the question of secession, military appropriations should be made, and a state coat of arms should be adopted. The governor also recommended that commissioners should be authorized to carry the word to other slaveholding states that Mississippi had no intention of submitting to Black Republican rule.[2]

Four days later, on November 30, the legislature authorized Governor Pettus to appoint commissioners to every slave state. These agents were to inform the states to which they were sent of Mississippi's forthcoming convention, and they were to seek the support of those states for whatever measures would promote the "common defense and safety" of the South.[3]

Pettus moved promptly to name commissioners. As a sign of the state's political unity in the face of danger, the governor chose men from the ranks of both the Democratic and Whig Parties, and in a matter of days, Mississippi's emissaries were fanning out across the South.[4] The unspoken task of every commissioner was to advance the cause of secession wherever he went.

Pettus was not the only governor to name commissioners in the tense weeks following Lincoln's victory. In early December, Governor Andrew B. Moore of Alabama decided on his own initiative to send commissioners out as well. Consultations were necessary, Moore believed, because of the unprecedented crisis facing the South. The Republican Party aimed at nothing less than "the destruction of the institution of slavery," Moore insisted, and "the peace, interests, security and honor of the slaveholding states" were imperiled.[5] The Alabama Convention would meet in January 1861 to decide on a course of action for the state; in the interim, commissioners could work to promote disunion elsewhere in the region.

Like Mississippi's Pettus, Moore, a strong Southern rights Democrat, named both Democratic firebrands and Whig moderates to represent the state.[6] The governor clearly was attempting to signal that the sectional crisis had obliterated long-standing party loyalties and that all Alabamians were secessionists now. Alabama's commissioners, like their counterparts from Mississippi, were soon on the move.

On Thursday, December 13, 1860, twenty Southern senators and representatives met deep into the night at the Washington lodgings of Congressman Reuben Davis of Mississippi. They had gathered at Davis's invitation to assess the prospects for a congressional compromise that might satisfy the South and bring an end to the sectional crisis. Time was running out. South Carolina's convention was scheduled to assemble the next Monday, December 17, and the disunionist forces were mobilizing across the lower South. By eleven o'clock, when the meeting at Davis's rooms broke up, the group had reached unanimous agreement on a statement, which was promptly released to the press.

"The argument is exhausted," the Southern delegates insisted. "All hope of relief in the Union, through the agency of committees, Congressional legislation, or constitutional amendments is extinguished," they continued. "In our judgment the honor, safety and independence of the Southern people are to be found only in a Southern Confederacy—the inevitable result of separate State secession." The slave states, in short, should dissociate themselves as quickly as possible "from an unnatural and hostile Union." This document, labeled "A Southern Manifesto," drove one of the final nails into the coffin of constitutional unity and helped pave the way for the secession of South Carolina one week later.[7]

The "Southern Manifesto" was a ringing call for action, but there was little indication in the document as to why time was so short and secession was so necessary. It was left to others to explain why "the honor, safety and independence of the Southern people" were teetering on the brink of destruction in late 1860.

The challenge of providing such an explanation—of informing the Southern people of the dark forces threatening their region and driving their states to seek sanctuary outside the Union—was taken up by the secession commissioners. The Mississippi and Alabama commissioners led off, and others would soon follow.

The first wave of activity came in mid-December. In a span of four days, from December 17 to December 20, commissioners carried the secessionist gospel to four states across the South. The messages they delivered were, to some degree, tailored to meet the needs of their audiences. South Carolina, for example, did not need to be prodded in the direction of disunion. Radical forces were in firm control there, and all the commissioners really needed to do was to wish the South Carolinians Godspeed as they turned their backs on the Union. Other states presented more formidable difficulties. In places like Georgia, North Carolina, and Maryland—early stops on the commissioners' itineraries—secession was by no means assured. It was here—in Milledgeville, Raleigh, and Baltimore—that the commissioners first unlimbered their rhetorical artillery.

By the third week in December, South Carolina was poised on the brink of secession. The state's legislature had remained in session during the November presidential election so as to be able to respond at once in the event of a Republican victory. When word of that calamity reached the state, the General Assembly immediately authorized a convention to meet in Columbia on December 17 to decide the question of secession. South Carolina's two United States senators promptly resigned their seats, and the state legislature prepared to arm a defense force of 10,000 men. "The tea has been thrown overboard, the revolution of 1860 has been initiated," commented the state's most radical newspaper, the *Charleston Mercury*.[8]

On Friday, December 14, John Archer Elmore, Alabama's commissioner to South Carolina, arrived in Columbia. Elmore was an apt choice for this assignment. He was a native South Carolinian who had graduated with distinction from South Carolina College and had

read law in the state before moving to Alabama. His former law part-
ner in Montgomery was none other than William L. Yancey, one of
the South's most outspoken fire-eaters and a leader of secessionist
forces in Alabama. By 1860 Elmore was a committed Southern rights
Democrat and an ardent disunionist—a perfect fit for a state like
South Carolina where secessionist enthusiasm was reaching a fever
pitch.[9]

The next day, December 15, Charles Edward Hooker, the commissioner from Mississippi, joined Elmore in the South Carolina
capital. Hooker was also a native of South Carolina, but he had pur-
sued his higher education outside the state, first at Randolph-Macon
College in Virginia and then at Harvard, where he had studied law.
After settling in Mississippi, he became a prominent lawyer, was an
active and vocal member of the Democratic Party, and was elected to
the state legislature in 1859.[10] One Mississippi newspaper described
him during this legislative campaign as "a fire-eater of the most ultra
disunion stripe," again an excellent choice for a mission to South
Carolina.[11]

The South Carolina press welcomed the arrival of these two commissioners, but one newspaper in the capital cautioned the two men
not to try to slow the disunionist tide engulfing the state. "In this
hour of trial, when the die is cast, when action has already been re-
solved upon by the people, and the delegates are meeting only to
record the great popular decree," wrote the editor of the *Columbia
Guardian,* "it is not the part of considerate friendship to paralyze their
arm by whispering warning or disapproving sounds in their ears."
The state "gladly receives the cheering sounds of approval," he continued, but South Carolina would reject "appeals for delay, when delay is dishonor."[12]

The editor need not have worried. Neither Elmore nor Hooker

had the slightest intention of doing anything other than telling the convention delegates exactly what they wanted to hear.

The election of Lincoln was "an avowed declaration of war upon the institutions, the rights and the interests of the South," Elmore told the convention on the evening of December 17. Under these circumstances "there should be no hesitation—no faltering and no delay upon the part of this Convention." South Carolina's "Ordinance of Secession . . . should take effect at once," Elmore advised, to loud and sustained applause. Immediate secession would "give the cause strength not only in Alabama, but in other states united with her in sentiment." [13]

Hooker, who followed Elmore to the convention platform, agreed wholeheartedly with the commissioner from Alabama. "I know, that the interest and welfare, and destiny and fate of South Carolina, is the interest, welfare, destiny and fate of Mississippi," Hooker said. It was time for South Carolina to "snatch her star from the galaxy in which it has hitherto mingled and plant her flag earliest in the breech of battle, sustaining revolution by the bold hearts and willing arms of her people." [14]

Three days later, after the convention had relocated to Charleston following an outbreak of smallpox in Columbia, the delegates acted. On December 20, 1860, the South Carolina Convention adopted an ordinance cutting all ties with the United States of America.

Elmore and Hooker had responded to the mood of the hour and promised that their states would follow South Carolina's lead at the earliest possible moment. This was all they really needed to do. A much more difficult task faced Mississippi's commissioner to Georgia, William L. Harris. Strong Unionist sentiment still existed in some parts of that state, and prominent Georgia politicians like Benjamin H. Hill and Herschel V. Johnson were urging caution, even in

the wake of Lincoln's election. Harris, a well-known Mississippi orator, would need to present the strongest possible argument when his
chance came to make the case for secession.

Harris was a native Georgian who had graduated from that state's
university in 1825. He had read law and been admitted to the Georgia
bar in 1826 by a special act of the state legislature—an action required
because Harris, who was born in 1807, had not reached his twenty-
first birthday. After practicing law for a number of years in Georgia,
he had moved in 1837 to Columbus, Mississippi, where he became a
leader in Whig politics. He was elected a circuit court judge in 1853,
he played a major role in rewriting the Mississippi legal code in 1856,
and he was elected to Mississippi's supreme court, the High Court of
Errors and Appeals, in 1858. President James Buchanan offered Harris
a seat on the United States Supreme Court in 1860, but Harris declined the nomination because he thought mounting sectional tension was likely to result in disunion. Harris had an outstanding reputation as a member of the legal profession, and Congressman Reuben
Davis considered him "a great thinker and debater." He was a natural
choice when Governor Pettus was looking for someone who might
influence the way Georgia would calculate the value of the Union
during the secession crisis.[15]

Judge Harris spoke to a joint session of the Georgia General Assembly at high noon on Monday, December 17, 1860, the same day
that Elmore and Hooker addressed the South Carolina Convention
(for the full text of Harris's address, see the Appendix). Harris began
his address, as many of the commissioners would do, by giving his
audience a history lesson. In Harris's case this review of Northern
"outrages" committed against the South was relatively brief. After a
cursory sketch of the North's failure during the 1850s "to yield to us
our constitutional rights in relation to slave property," he moved to
the heart of his argument.

The triumph of the Republican Party in the recent presidential election revealed a North "more defiant and more intolerant than ever before," Harris insisted. "They have demanded, and now demand, equality between the white and negro races, under our Constitution; equality in representation, equality in the right of suffrage, equality in the honors and emoluments of office, equality in the social circle, equality in the rights of matrimony," he said. The new administration coming to power on March 4 promised "freedom to the slave, but eternal degradation for you and for us."

Every other issue paled in comparison to the Republican threat to the South's racial order. "Our fathers made this a government for the white man, rejecting the negro, as an ignorant, inferior, barbarian race, incapable of self-government, and not, therefore, entitled to be associated with the white man upon terms of civil, political, or social equality," Harris maintained. Lincoln's administration was determined "to overturn and strike down this great feature of our Union . . . and to substitute in its stead their new theory of the universal equality of the black and white races."

Under these circumstances the choice for the South was clear: "This *new union* with Lincoln Black Republicans and free negroes, *without slavery*; or, slavery under our old constitutional bond of union, *without* Lincoln Black Republicans, or free negroes either, to molest us." If white Southerners wanted to avoid "submission to negro equality," then "*secession* is inevitable," he told the Georgia legislators. Judge Harris closed his brief address with this peroration:

> Sink or swim, live or die, survive or perish, the part of Mississippi is chosen, *she will never submit* to the principles and policy of this Black Republican Administration.
>
> She had rather see the last of her race, men, women and children, immolated in one common funeral pile [pyre], than see them

subjected to the degradation of civil, political and social equality with the negro race.[16]

In response to Harris's speech, the Georgia house and senate adopted a joint resolution condemning the Northern people, press, and pulpit for supporting a political party "organized . . . for the avowed purpose of destroying the institution of slavery, and consequently spreading ruin and desolation among the people in every portion of the states where it exists." The legislature also ordered the printing of a thousand copies of his speech.[17] The *Athens Southern Banner* called the date Harris addressed the legislature "the greatest day of the session."[18]

Although Commissioners Elmore, Hooker, and Harris all spoke on the same day, it was Judge Harris who set the tone for what was to follow. The racial themes that he struck in his speech would echo through the statements of other commissioners as they spread out across the South in late 1860 and early 1861.

On December 18, 1860, the *New York Times* noted that Secretary of the Interior Jacob Thompson had passed through Baltimore the previous day on his way to North Carolina. "The object of his visit is unascertained," the report added.

The *Times* did not have to wait long to learn why this member of President James Buchanan's cabinet was sailing down the Chesapeake. "Mr. Secretary Thompson . . . goes as Commissioner from the State of Mississippi to the State of North Carolina," the *Times* reported with considerable dismay on December 20. "Secretary Thompson has entered openly into the secession service, while professing still to serve the Federal authority."

Indeed he had. Thompson, a well-known Mississippi Democrat, was one of several Washington figures named in late 1860 to serve as secession commissioners to slave states in the upper South. Proximity sped the process of persuasion, and Congressmen Jabez Lamar Monroe Curry and David Clopton, both Alabama Democrats and sitting members of the United States House of Representatives, would soon be on the road as well.

Jacob Thompson, born in North Carolina in 1810, had maintained close ties to that state over the years. In the 1830s, after graduating from the University of North Carolina, he had relocated to Mississippi where he developed a lucrative law practice and launched a highly successful political career. He served six consecutive terms in Congress, from 1839 to 1851, before taking his position in the Buchanan administration in 1857.[19]

In a speech given in Raleigh in 1859, Thompson had denounced both Northern Republicans who spoke of an "irrepressible conflict" between the sections and Southern ultras who favored reopening the slave trade to Africa. Thompson told his North Carolina audience on this occasion that he would rally under the national banner if the "restless reformers" advocating a renewed African slave trade gained a foothold in the South.[20] Now, in December 1860, he was arriving in the North Carolina capital as a standard-bearer for the secessionist cause.

On December 18 Secretary Thompson met with Governor John W. Ellis immediately upon his arrival in Raleigh. The two men had a friendly meeting, and that night Thompson sat in his hotel room and committed his thoughts to paper. His open letter to the governor, laid before the North Carolina legislature on December 20 and published in the *Raleigh State Journal* two days later, resonated with the same dire warnings Judge Harris had just sounded in Georgia.

The "Irrepressible Conflict" crowd had finally gained ascendancy in the North, Thompson wrote, and the slave South now faced "common humiliation and ruin." Lincoln's inauguration on March 4 would bring to power "a majority trained from infancy to hate our people and their institutions." Soon this Black Republican abolition horde would be proclaiming "that 'Freedom is triumphant' and that 'slavery is overthrown,'" Thompson claimed. Our "common Government will be revolutionized," he continued, and "it will be perverted into an engine for the destruction of our domestic institutions, and the subjugation of our people." It was the simple dictate of wisdom, Thompson concluded, "that all questions arising out of the institution of slavery, should be settled now and settled forever." [21]

Thompson's prophecy of emancipation, humiliation, subjugation, and ruin runs through the commissioners' messages like a scarlet thread. The slave South was standing on the brink of a racial abyss, they insisted. Such was the clear warning of two speeches given in the upper South on December 19 and December 20—the day before, and the day of, South Carolina's secession.

On the evening of December 19, Judge Alexander Hamilton Handy, Mississippi's commissioner to Maryland, rose to address a raucous crowd of over 1,500 people crammed into Maryland Institute Hall in Baltimore. The previous day Handy had gone to Annapolis for what turned out to be a singularly unsuccessful meeting with Maryland's Unionist governor, Thomas H. Hicks. Handy had urged the governor to summon a special meeting of the state legislature "for the purpose of counseling with the constituted authorities of the State of Mississippi" on how best to defend "the safety and rights of the Southern States." Hicks knew a secessionist stalking-horse when he saw one, and the governor had flatly refused to call the legislature into session. [22] Handy was determined to take his case directly to the people of Maryland, however, and his Baltimore speech was a first step in that direction.

Judge Handy, a native Marylander who had moved to Mississippi in the 1830s, served with William L. Harris on the High Court of

Errors and Appeals. Like Harris, Judge Handy had become a staunch secessionist by 1860.[23] And, again like Harris, Judge Handy firmly believed that the racial fate of the South was hanging in the balance.

The election of Abraham Lincoln had plunged the country into "a state of revolution," Handy told the Baltimore audience, and for good reason; the Republican platform revealed a clear intent "to overthrow the constitution, and subvert the rights of the South." Handy was not talking about abstract "rights" here; he was referring to the right "by which one man can own property in his fellow man." To the "black republican" claim that "slavery is a sin before God and the world," Handy posited a counterclaim: "Slavery was ordained by God and sanctioned by humanity." Southerners "would not give up their slaves" because to do so would turn "the beautiful cotton fields" of their region into "barren wastes," he said.

The primary thrust of Handy's argument was not an economic one, however, as he quickly made clear. "The first act of the black republican party will be to exclude slavery from all the Territories, the District [of Columbia], the arsenals and the forts, by the action of the general government," he predicted. "That would be a recognition that slavery is a sin, and confine the institution to its present limits," he went on. "The moment that slavery is pronounced a moral evil—a sin—by the general government, that moment the safety of the rights of the South will be entirely gone."

The Lincoln administration would not stop with these initial moves against slavery, however. Handy was convinced that the Republicans would "repeal the laws which prohibit circulation of incendiary documents, so that they may be sent among the slaves to excite them against their masters." The South would be infiltrated with Republican agents provocateurs—"postmasters and other officials"—who would "excite the slave to cut the throat of his master." Thus the only way for the South to prevent widespread slave insurrection, the only means of self-preservation, was immediate secession. The Southern states "must take action before Lincoln comes to power, so that they will be out of the power of his myrmidons," he insisted. "This question of slavery must be settled now or never," and the political unrest of the past thirty years had to end. The slavery agitation was "a festering sore upon the body politic," Handy concluded. It was time to try "amputation" to bring the patient "to a healthy state."[24]

The day after Judge Handy spoke in Baltimore, two Alabamians, Isham W. Garrott and Robert Hardy Smith, addressed a joint session of the North Carolina legislature. The two men who carried Alabama's commission to Raleigh that December were both natives of North Carolina who had settled in Alabama in the 1830s to practice law. Both men had served in the Alabama legislature as Whigs, and both had crossed political swords with powerful Democratic figures in the state. Robert Hardy Smith was a longtime opponent of William L. Yancey, and Isham W. Garrott had begun his legislative career as an antagonist of Andrew B. Moore, the man who, as governor, named Garrott one of the state's commissioners in 1860.[25] Governor Moore, once again, was sending a message that Alabamians of every political stripe were now united in the face of the threat posed by Lincoln, Black Republicanism, and all the other abolitionist elements that might be gathering in the North.

Garrott and Smith saw the darkest of days ahead for the slave South. Their North Carolina message was filled with forebodings that grew increasingly grim as time stretched into the future. Lincoln's election meant, first of all, that Southern slaveholders would be excluded from the territories, that no new slave states could ever be created, and that the South would inevitably face political emasculation. But that was not the worst of it. The North "proposes to impair the value of slave property in the States by unfriendly legislation," they claimed, "and by these means to render the institution itself dangerous to us, and compel us, as slaves increase, to abandon it, or be doomed to a servile war." The Gulf States were particularly vulnerable, they believed, and their region anticipated "utter ruin and degradation" under Republican rule. "Alabama has at least eight slaves to every square mile of her tillable soil," they warned. "This population outstrips any race on the globe in the rapidity of its increase; and if the slaves now in Alabama are to be restricted within the present limits, doubling as they do once in less than thirty years, the [white] children are now born who will be compelled to flee from the land of their birth, and from the slaves their parents have toiled to acquire as an inheritance for them, or to submit to the degradation of being reduced to an equality with them, and all its attendant horrors."

Garrott and Smith offered the North Carolinians friendly reassurance about one matter, however. "The non-slaveholding States, while declaring that we shall not expand, and that thereby we shall be crushed by our slave population, are charging upon us a design to reopen the African slave trade," they warned. "The charge is a slander upon our people, and a reflection upon their intelligence." The slaveholders of the lower South "feel no desire to depreciate the value of their own property, nor to demoralize their slaves by throwing among them savages and cannibals," they wrote. "They will look, as heretofore, to the redundant slave population of the more Northern of their associated sister States of the South for such additions to their negroes as their wants may require."

A shared economic interest in slavery, and the internal slave trade, was a subject of some importance, but it was by no means the central issue. As they made clear throughout their address, Garrott and Smith were convinced that the controversy between the North and the South turned on one thing and one thing alone—the issue of race.

They ended their address with a call for Southern unity. "The sectional strife has now been conducted with increasing rancor for more than twenty years," they argued, and Southerners "have grown tired of the controversy, and can see no good in prolonging the quarrel, and no way to end it in the Union." The time for secession had arrived. "Submission would but invite new and greater aggressions, until Alabama would become a despised and degraded province." It was no time for "a divided South," they concluded; the moment had come for North Carolina to join Alabama in protecting the South and slavery from the "desecrating touch" of Northern fanaticism.[26]

This address by Garrott and Smith was the final act in the first phase of the commissioners' activities across the South. Over the four-day period from December 17 to December 20, agents from Alabama and Mississippi had carried their message to slave states stretching from Maryland to Georgia. Their public statements revealed the core of the secession persuasion gripping the Deep South in the weeks between Lincoln's election and South Carolina's vote to dissolve all ties to the Union. December 20, 1860, marked a critical turning point in the sectional controversy. The same day Garrott and Smith were urging North Carolina to join the lower South in resisting Yankee aggression, the South Carolina Convention passed its ordinance of secession. After that fateful decision, the South faced a new set of dangers. The next wave of secession commissioners responded to this crisis with a fresh burst of rhetoric that left no doubt as to where the cause of the South truly lay.

CHAPTER 3

The South Carolinians

THE vote in the South Carolina Convention was unanimous. On the afternoon of December 20, 1860, the delegates adopted South Carolina's Ordinance of Secession by a tally of 169 to 0. That evening, a formal signing of the document took place in Institute Hall in Charleston, and an immense crowd gathered to witness the event. At the conclusion of this solemn two-hour ceremony, the convention president, David F. Jamison, announced that South Carolina was now "an Independent Commonwealth." The audience roared its approval, and celebrants thronged Charleston's streets deep into the night.[1]

The previous day, December 19, Isaac W. Hayne, the state attorney general and a convention delegate, had raised the issue of sending commissioners to other slave states. Hayne's move was a bit premature. He called for the commissioners to carry a copy of South Carolina's Ordinance of Secession with them before that document had even been approved, so his commissioner proposal, along with his suggestion that the United States Constitution serve as the basis for organizing a new "Provisional Government" for the seceded states, was referred to the convention's Committee on Relations with the Slaveholding States of North America.[2]

On December 24 the *Charleston Mercury* enthusiastically endorsed the idea of putting a new Southern government in place as quickly as possible. "The Convention now sitting in South Carolina, and all the other Conventions which shall assemble to dissolve the existing Union, have the power . . . of speedily organizing a Confederacy," the editor wrote. "Uncertainty and delay are dangerous," he warned, and other seceding states would be looking to South Carolina for leadership. The editorial suggested a meeting in Montgomery, Alabama, in early February "to form a Constitution for a Southern Confederacy, and to put the same into operation."

The *Mercury* was the organ of Robert Barnwell Rhett, one of South Carolina's most outspoken secessionists. Rhett was also a convention delegate and the chairman of the Committee on Relations with the Slaveholding States.[3] Attorney General Hayne's ideas came back to the floor of the convention on December 26. Rhett's committee proposed the immediate selection of commissioners and their dispatch to other Southern states that had announced they would call conventions. South Carolina's agents, like their counterparts from Alabama and Mississippi, were to do everything in their power to advance the cause of secession, but they were given an additional charge as well. They were to propose a meeting in Montgomery on February 13, 1861, to draft a constitution for a Confederate States of America.[4]

The convention acted swiftly to implement these recommendations. On December 29 the delegates endorsed the idea of appointing commissioners, and they supported most of the committee's other recommendations as well; the only significant change was to leave open the time and place for the meeting of the Constitutional Convention.[5]

The delegates then proceeded to name commissioners, and by January 2 the first phase of this process was completed. The South Carolina Convention appointed seven commissioners at this time:

to Georgia, Florida, Alabama, Mississippi, Louisiana, Arkansas, and Texas. Virginia and North Carolina were subsequently added to the list.[6]

The day after their appointment by the convention, the South Carolina commissioners met in Charleston to plan strategy. They agreed to suggest Montgomery as the site for a constitutional convention. Convenient rail and river access and good hotel accommodations recommended the Alabama capital, and the fact that Montgomery was the home of William L. Yancey made it doubly attractive to the South Carolinians. They also decided to propose the earliest possible date for this meeting—the first Monday in February. South Carolina's commissioners were now ready to sow the seeds of revolution across the Deep South.[7]

Andrew Pickens Calhoun, South Carolina's commissioner to Alabama, arrived in Montgomery on the evening of January 6. The Alabama Convention was scheduled to open at noon the next day, and the city was jammed with people, but the press singled out Commissioner Calhoun for special mention. As the duly accredited representative of the sovereign and independent state of South Carolina, it was hardly surprising that his presence was noted in newspapers as far away as New York City.[8]

Andrew Calhoun was the son of a famous father. As the child of John C. Calhoun, he might have been expected to play a prominent role in South Carolina politics, but such had not been the case. Andrew had devoted himself primarily to a life on the land. In 1835, at the age of twenty-three, he had moved with a sizable slave force to the Alabama Black Belt and over the years had become one of the most prosperous cotton planters in his region. Several years after his father's death in 1850, Andrew returned to his native South Carolina up-country. In 1855 he sold a portion of his Alabama lands and purchased Fort Hill, the Calhoun family estate in Abbeville District. In his political views he was a strong states' rights Democrat and a committed secessionist, but his public activities in the 1850s had centered largely around the South Carolina Agricultural Society—an organization he helped found and one that, beginning in 1856, he served for a number of years as president.[9]

Despite his relative absence from the political arena, there was no question where Calhoun stood on the issues of the day. His ties to Alabama certainly recommended him for his mission to Montgomery, but so did his conviction that Lincoln's election was an unmitigated disaster for the South. He revealed his thoughts in his presidential address to the South Carolina Agricultural Society on the evening of November 13, 1860, exactly one week after Lincoln's victory and well before he was dispatched to Alabama.

Calhoun gave this speech in the State Capitol in Columbia, which was an appropriate setting for what he was about to say. He made almost no reference to agriculture in his remarks. Instead, he launched into a passionate attack on the North for embracing an "Abolitionist" president and for threatening the South with "political and social destruction." Republicans would inaugurate "a depraved Government" on March 4, he insisted, and they would seek "to seduce the poor, ignorant and stupid nature of the negro in the midst of his home and happiness." Calhoun drew a chilling parallel between the impact of Republican abolitionist propaganda on the slaves of the South and the effect that French Revolutionary rhetoric—specifically the slogan "liberty, equality and fraternity"—had had on the slave population of Haiti. "Well, the [Haitian] negro heard the ill omened words, and he, born in Africa, the slave, whose head was always in danger, perhaps to repair some skull-built wall of a kinky-headed chief, who, hunted down, captured, famished in his native land, could only view his change as a blessed one—he, too, arose, with all the fury of the beast, and scenes were then enacted over a comparatively few planters, that the white fiends [of the North] would delight to see re-enacted now with us." The only way to save the South from a similar fate, he concluded, was "disentanglement from the North," a separation that had to be "complete, thorough and radical." [10]

Edmund Ruffin, Virginia's leading secessionist, was in the audience that night and pronounced Calhoun's address a "very good composition . . . entirely applicable to the present political crisis, and situation of the Southern states." [11] According to the local press, the speech "was listened to with marked attention, and received with loud applause." [12]

Calhoun's message to the Alabama Convention, delivered on January 8, 1861, lacked some of the rhetorical fireworks of his Agricultural Society address, but the main point he made in Montgomery was the same one he had offered in Columbia eight weeks earlier: the election of a "Black Republican" to the presidency threatened South Carolina with "degradation and annihilation." Even under these dire circumstances, South Carolina had no desire to take the lead in dismembering the Union, Calhoun maintained. But "a combination of accidental causes" had thrust his state into a position to act first, and act it did. South Carolina's "submission" to "the measured approach of despotism" was out of the question, he observed; the legislature was in session when word of Lincoln's election arrived, the call for a convention went out, and "an up-heaving of the people" took place. "No leader or leaders could have resisted it, or stemmed its impetuosity," Calhoun claimed, and secession quickly followed.

After presenting the convention with a copy of South Carolina's secession ordinance, Calhoun asked Alabama to join "in the formation of a Southern Confederacy." As the commissioners had agreed before they left Charleston, he proposed the first week in February as the appropriate time for a constitutional convention and suggested Montgomery as a possible site. "A common cause unites Alabama and South Carolina and the other cotton States," Calhoun maintained. He concluded his speech with the impassioned insistence that South Carolinians "from the mountains to the sea-board . . . will 'die free-men rather than live slaves.'"[13]

A reporter in the audience noted that despite "the rule which had been passed suppressing applause, the closing part of his address was received with the most vociferous shouts of approbation, from members of the convention, not less than outsiders."[14] When Alabama left the Union three days later, the secession ordinance contained a resolution inviting the slave states to a convention in Montgomery on February 4, 1861.[15]

As South Carolina's commissioner to Florida, the convention chose the man Horace Greeley had labeled "the philosopher of the new African slave trade."[16] Leonidas W. Spratt, one of the most strident secessionist voices in South Carolina, had launched his campaign to reopen the human traffic from Africa in the columns of the *Charleston Southern Standard,* a paper he began editing in 1853. A native South Carolinian, Spratt had graduated from South Carolina College—a veritable school for secessionists—before moving to Florida, where he practiced law and then served as a probate judge in the Apalachicola area. In 1850, at the age of thirty-two, Spratt had returned to South Carolina, had set up a law practice in Charleston, and had taken up the slave trade cause. His most famous legal battle came when he successfully defended the crew of the brig *Echo,* an American slaver captured by a United States Navy vessel off Cuba and brought into Charleston harbor in 1858. Spratt served in the South Carolina legislature that called the secession convention in 1860, and he was elected as a delegate to that body.[17] His Florida connections unquestionably played a role in his selection as commissioner, but so did his politics. Florida stood with South Carolina and Mississippi at the apex of Southern radicalism in the tumultuous weeks following Lincoln's election.

In contrast with commissioners like Mississippi's Jacob Thompson, who bemoaned the triumph of the "Irrepressible Conflict" school in the North, Spratt embraced the rise of Republicans to power. "Within this government two societies have become developed," he told the Florida convention on January 7. "The one is the society of one race, the other of two races. The one is based on free labor, the other slave labor. The one is braced together by but the two great relations of life—the relations of husband and wife, and parent and child; the other by the three relations of husband and wife, parent and child, and master and slave. The one embodies the social principle that equality is the right of man; the other, the social principle that equality is not the right of man, but the right of equals only." Two distinct and profoundly different civilizations had thus emerged in the United States, "and the contest was inevitable," Spratt claimed. "There is and must be an irrepressible conflict between them, and it were best to realize the truth."

Spratt went to considerable lengths to defend South Carolina against the charge that the state had acted precipitously in the current crisis. In his view "an overt act" of Lincolnian despotism was not a necessary precondition for secession. "To slaves it may be a question whether the repetition of the lash can be endured," he went on to say, "but to freemen the only question is as to the assumption to inflict the lash, and that determined, it could little matter whether there should be one lash more or less." White South Carolinians had seized the moment because the malicious intent of "the Black Republican party" was clear. "We knew that the men of the South were too instructed, and too brave, to submit to the severities of final subjugation," he added.

Like all the South Carolina commissioners, Spratt worked hard in his speech to promote the speedy calling of a constitutional convention and the organization of a provisional government for the seceding states. Early February was none too soon for such activity, he argued. South Carolinians had deliberately "offered our state as the battle-ground for Southern rights" and had sought "a pre eminence of danger" in order to unite the region in resistance to Northern aggression, Spratt concluded. By leading the procession of Southern states out of the Union, South Carolina had "erected at least one nationality under the authority of which the powers of slavery may stand in that fearful contest for existence which at some time or other was bound to come." [18]

The ubiquitous Edmund Ruffin, in Tallahassee to witness Florida's act of secession, listened to Spratt's address and found it "a logical and able argument." [19] The Florida Convention passed its Ordinance of Secession three days later, on January 10, and swiftly agreed to the South Carolina plan for organizing a new government. [20]

A central purpose of Spratt's mission to Florida, like that of Calhoun to Alabama, was to ensure that South Carolina would not remain isolated and vulnerable at the van of the secessionist movement. Too often their state had stood alone in defense of the rights of the slave South, but the dangers inherent in such an exposed position were many times greater in late 1860 and early 1861 than at any time in the past.

Tensions were mounting in Charleston that could explode at any moment. On December 26 Major Robert Anderson had shifted his small Federal garrison from land-based Fort Moultrie to Fort Sumter in the middle of the harbor, a move the South Carolina authorities considered highly provocative. On January 9, two days after Commissioner Spratt spoke to the Florida Convention, South Carolina batteries opened fire on the *Star of the West,* an unarmed Federal vessel attempting to bring supplies and troop reinforcements to Fort Sumter, and forced the relief ship to exit Charleston harbor.[21] War seemed a distinct possibility, and South Carolina could ill afford to enter such a conflict without allies. Spratt, Calhoun, and the other South Carolina commissioners crafted their messages both to defend their state against charges of undue haste and to secure the speedy cooperation of every slave state holding a convention in January 1861. Secession, a Confederate government, and military assistance were their goals. South Carolina's fate was hanging in the balance during the opening weeks of the new year as its commissioners made their way across the Deep South.

South Carolina's campaign for Southern unity continued throughout the month of January. On January 11 former congressman Armistead Burt, commissioner from "the Republic of South Carolina," told the Mississippi Convention that his state had seceded because the Republican Party clearly intended "to uproot our institutions, and desolate the Southern country." South Carolinians "had determined, with one mind, that there was nothing so intolerable as degradation," Burt added. After explaining that South Carolina had had no desire to lead the secessionist parade, he asked Mississippi to send delegates to the convention meeting in Montgomery in early February.[22] The Mississippians, who had passed their Ordinance of Secession two days before Burt spoke, promptly accepted his invitation.[23]

During the following two weeks, James L. Orr, commissioner to Georgia, and John L. Manning, commissioner to Louisiana, delivered similar messages and saw the states to which they were sent quickly fall in line behind South Carolina.

Orr, a veteran South Carolina Democratic congressman and former Speaker of the United States House of Representatives, had a well-deserved reputation for political moderation. A longtime foe of Robert Barnwell Rhett, Leonidas W. Spratt, and other radical elements in his native state, Orr had strenuously opposed the move to reopen the slave trade and had not joined the secessionist ranks until almost the eleventh hour. Only in the spring of 1860 with the breakup of the national Democratic Party did Orr come to accept the inevitability of disunion. A key element in his conversion was his fear for the fate of the white race under Republican rule.[24]

On November 23, 1860, less than three weeks after Lincoln's election, Orr had outlined his views to a mass meeting in Pendleton, South Carolina. The abolition of slavery would produce ruinous competition between the races, he said, a struggle that would force the white man to enter the poorhouse or flee the country. Emancipation also threatened white South Carolinians with the specter of racial equality—a subject Orr was loath even to mention. He vowed that he "*never would submit* to such equality, equality at the ballot box and jury box, and at the witness stand." With this sort of threat looming over their heads, the white people of his state had no choice but to seek safety outside the Union.[25]

Orr's comments to the Georgia delegates came on January 17, 1861, the second day of the convention. After issuing the usual disclaimer about South Carolina's supposedly "too precipitate action," he launched into a vitriolic attack on "the Black-Republican party" and everything it stood for. The South "had suffered indignities and insults until they were no longer tolerable," Orr proclaimed. The North was firmly in the grip "of a blind and relentless fanaticism," and a Lincoln administration would lead inevitably to "southern degradation and dishonor." Orr, who described himself as a "conservative and Union-loving man," saw no way out short of secession. The idea of a Montgomery meeting on February 4 was gaining momentum, and Orr urged the Georgians to take part.[26] According to press reports, the "immense crowd" in attendance greeted Orr's speech "with a wildness and an enthusiasm, that told well, for the effect being produced by this gifted and honored son of Carolina."[27]

Disunionist forces were in firm control of the Georgia Convention, and Orr did not have to wait long to see the results of this strength. Georgia seceded on January 19, two days after his speech, and agreed to send delegates to Montgomery.[28]

Commissioner James L. Manning's experience in Louisiana closely paralleled that of Orr in Georgia. Manning, who had served as governor of South Carolina from 1852 to 1854, was one of the richest planters in the state. He had extensive landholdings in both South Carolina and Louisiana, and his slave force numbered in the hundreds.[29]

Louisiana newspapers printed only a brief synopsis of his remarks before that state's convention on January 25, but it is clear from these reports that he followed the South Carolina script closely. The imminent threat posed by the South's "avowed enemies"—"the Black Republicans"—more than justified the "immediate action" of his state, Manning maintained, and he had come to Baton Rouge "to ask the cooperation of Louisiana in the formation of a Southern Confederacy."[30] Louisiana's secession came the next day, January 26, and the convention committed the state to full participation in the Montgomery Constitutional Convention.[31] Manning, like the other South Carolina commissioners, had done his job well.

The final South Carolina mission in this initial wave of activity was former congressman John McQueen's journey to Texas. McQueen, a Bennettsville, South Carolina, lawyer, had served in Congress throughout the decade of the 1850s. His political views were at the radical end of the South Carolina spectrum, and he was one of the congressmen who had signed the "Southern Manifesto" on December 13, 1860, calling for the immediate secession of all the slaveholding states.[32] McQueen and the rest of his state's congressional delegation were still in Washington a week later when South Carolina left the Union. The next day, December 21, he and his colleagues resigned their seats in the House and prepared to head home.[33]

Before he could leave Washington, however, McQueen received a letter from a group of Richmond civic leaders inviting him and his fellow South Carolinians to stop off in the Virginia capital for a testimonial dinner where the "free, sovereign, independent State" of South Carolina could be appropriately toasted and celebrated.

McQueen graciously declined this invitation; his wife was ill, and most of his colleagues had already departed. But he took pains in his reply to thank the Richmonders for their expression of solidarity with his home state. "I have never doubted what Virginia would do when the alternatives present themselves to her intelligent and gallant people, to choose between an association with her Southern sisters, and the dominion of a people who have chosen their leader"—Abraham Lincoln—"upon the single idea that the African is equal to the Anglo-Saxon, and with the purpose of placing our slaves on [a position of] equality with ourselves and our friends of every condition," he wrote. "We, of South Carolina, hope soon to greet you in a Southern Confederacy, where white men shall rule our destinies, and from which we may transmit to our posterity the rights, privileges and honor left us by our ancestors." [34]

Commissioner McQueen struck this same chord when he addressed the Texas Convention on February 1, 1861. "Lincoln was elected by a sectional vote, whose platform was that of the Black Republican party and whose policy was to be the abolition of slavery upon this continent and the elevation of our own slaves to an equality with ourselves and our children," he told the delegates. As a consequence, South Carolina had "struck the blow" for secession, and McQueen invited the Texans to join the rest of the cotton states at Montgomery on February 4.[35] The convention passed a secession ordinance that same day and prepared to join the Confederacy.[36]

McQueen was, needless to say, delighted with the swift action of the Texas body. For a state facing "three distinct classes of most unprincipled enemies . . . , Indians, Mexicans and Abolitionists," the Texans had acted with remarkable courage and fortitude, he reported back to South Carolina. He predicted that Texas would "never again be united, in any union whatever, with a non-slaveholding or fanatical people."[37]

The South Carolina commissioners had spoken with a remarkably unified voice in the early weeks of 1861. Some of that unity, it seems clear, was planned. South Carolina's headlong rush to secede required some explanation and justification, particularly in light of the state's well-deserved reputation as the most radical of all the slaveholding states. In like manner, the need to rally the South in the face of possible Northern military action made it imperative that the commissioners advance the idea of a constitutional convention and the rapid organization of a new provisional government. As the *Charleston Mercury* had noted on December 24, indecision and delay were dangerous indulgences in this postsecession moment of peril. The call for the Montgomery meeting in early February had grown directly out of the commissioners' joint consultations on January 3 before they dispersed across the lower South.

There is no way to know whether they moved beyond these two points at this Charleston caucus. But over and over again, they used the same key words and called up the same vivid images. "Submission" to the "blind and ruthless fanaticism" of the North was not an option because submission meant acquiescence in the certain destruction of slavery. Emancipation, in turn, would bring "degradation," "final subjugation," and "annihilation" to the white South. The "Black Republicans"—this label never varied—were determined, as Armistead Burt put it, "to uproot our institutions, and desolate the Southern country."

The racial content of these images was crystal clear. John Mc-Queen expressed the key point as well as anyone when he spoke in Austin at the conclusion of the commissioners' January travels. It was unthinkable that South Carolinians would accept a president bent on "the abolition of slavery . . . and the elevation of our own slaves to an equality with ourselves and our children."

CHAPTER 4

The Alabamians

ALABAMA'S commissioners redoubled their efforts in the weeks following the secession of South Carolina. Their communications took on a new urgency as state after state across the lower South, including their own, plunged into the murky waters of secession. By February 1 seven Deep South states—South Carolina, Mississippi, Florida, Alabama, Georgia, Louisiana, and Texas—had left the Union. The task at hand, the commissioners well knew, was to bring the rest of the slave South into the fold.

Christmas Day 1860 found Stephen Fowler Hale, Alabama's commissioner to Kentucky, in Nashville. He was making connections for Louisville, he wrote a friend, and expected to arrive in Frankfort, the Kentucky capital, the next day.[1]

Hale already knew what he wanted to say. Before he left Alabama he had made a few remarks to a political meeting in Greene County that revealed his thinking on the eve of his mission to Frankfort. There was no need "to wait for an overt act" of aggression from the Lincoln administration before seceding, Hale said. The election of the Republican ticket was, in and of itself, "a culmination of aggravated outrage, which no Southern patriot could mistake or fail to understand." Lincoln's minions had a clear goal: "The extinction of slavery." Hale called for "separate State secession" now, "Confederation afterwards." Republicans were already "arming their emissaries to cut the throats of Southern men, women, and children," he claimed, and it would be the height of folly to "wait . . . until Lincoln should have the army and navy at his command . . . to subjugate us."[2] Several days after making these comments in Greene County, Hale was named the state's commissioner to Kentucky by Alabama governor Albert B. Moore.[3]

Stephen Hale was returning as commissioner to the land of his birth. Born in Crittenden County, Kentucky, in 1816, he had received his formal education first at Cumberland University and then at the Lexington law school of Transylvania University. He moved to Alabama in 1837 and subsequently set up a law practice in Eutaw, a small town in Greene County, just south of Tuscaloosa in the western part of the state. Described by one acquaintance as "tall and lank, with a large and knotty head" and "somewhat eccentric in his manners," Hale was elected to the Alabama legislature in 1843, served in the Mexican War, ran unsuccessfully for Congress in 1853, and then was returned to the state legislature in 1857 and again in 1859. In addition to practicing law, Hale was engaged in small-scale planting and was the owner of a dozen slaves in 1860.[4] There was no question where Hale, a strong Southern rights Whig, stood on the question of secession. As he told the voters in Greene County, Alabama should secede now, confederate later.

The Kentucky legislature was not in session when Hale arrived in Frankfort on December 26, so he directed his efforts at the state's governor, Beriah Magoffin. The day after he reached the Kentucky capital, Hale wrote out his views on the crisis confronting the slave South. His December 27 letter to Governor Magoffin is one of the most remarkable documents of the secession crisis (for the full text of Hale's letter, see the Appendix).

Hale began by reviewing the constitutional justification for secession and the South's economic stake in slavery, "an institution
with which is bound up not only the wealth and prosperity of the
Southern people, but their very existence as a political community."
Yankee "fanaticism" had become "an unchained demon," Hale asserted, and Northern assaults on the South and its peculiar institution
had reached intolerable levels. "They attack us through their literature, in their schools, from the hustings, in their legislative halls,
through the public press, and even their courts of justice," he wrote.
The 1850s had witnessed a string of outrages—widespread refusal to
return fugitive slaves, bloody attacks on proslavery settlers in Kansas,
and finally John Brown's raid on Harpers Ferry, Virginia, at the end
of the decade.

The recent election of the Republican ticket was the final blow,
according to Hale, who was careful to mention Lincoln's vice-
presidential running mate, Hannibal Hamlin, by name; papers across
the South carried rumors during the secession crisis that, as the
Charleston Mercury put it, Hamlin "had negro blood in his veins
and . . . one of his children had kinky hair." It was now, Hale told the
governor, "the imperative duty of the Southern States to resume the
powers they had delegated to the Federal Government and interpose
their sovereignty for the protection of their citizens." Secession was
the only proper response to the Republican electoral triumph, which
Hale called "the last and crowning insult and outrage upon the people
of the South." Lincoln "stands forth as the representative of the fanaticism of the North," he continued, and the Republican Party
stood for "one dogma—the equality of the races, white and black."
The embrace of the Negro by the victorious Republicans had put
"the interest, honor, and safety" of Southern whites squarely on the
line, Hale insisted.

Up to this point in his letter, Hale used rather restrained language.

Debates over fine points of constitutional interpretation or the meaning of historical events were not generally conducted at fever pitch by any of the commissioners. But as he moved to the climax of his argument, Hale took the rhetorical gloves off.

Lincoln's election was "nothing less than an open declaration of war, for the triumph of this new theory of government destroys the property of the South, lays waste her fields, and inaugurates all the horrors of a San Domingo servile insurrection, consigning her citizens to assassinations and her wives and daughters to pollution and violation to gratify the lust of half-civilized Africans," Hale wrote. "The slave-holder and non-slave-holder must ultimately share the same fate; all be degraded to a position of equality with free negroes, stand side by side with them at the polls, and fraternize in all the social relations of life, or else there will be an eternal war of races, desolating the land with blood, and utterly wasting all the resources of the country."

What Southerner, Hale asked, "can without indignation and horror contemplate the triumph of negro equality, and see his own sons and daughters in the not distant future associating with free negroes upon terms of political and social equality?" Abolition would surely mean that "the two races would be continually pressing together" in the South, and under these circumstances "amalgamation or the extermination of the one or the other would be inevitable." Could "Southern men submit to such degradation and ruin?" Hale knew the answer: "God forbid that they should."

Hale drew a sharp contrast between the prospects of an independent South and its fate within the Union. "If we triumph, vindicate our rights, and maintain our institutions, a bright and joyous future lies before us," he insisted. "If we fail, the light of our civilization goes down in blood, our wives and our little ones will be driven from their homes by the light of our own dwellings, [and] the dark pall of barbarism must soon gather over our sunny land."

Secession would thus provide both the path to a glorious future and the only means by which "the heaven-ordained superiority of the white over the black race" could be maintained. And there was no time to waste. "Shall we wait until our enemies shall possess themselves of all the powers of the Government; until abolition judges are on the Supreme Court bench, abolition collectors at every port, and abolition postmasters in every town; secret mail agents traversing the whole land, and a subsidized press established in our midst to demoralize our people?" The answer was obvious. "Alabama most respectfully urges upon the people and authorities of Kentucky the startling truth that submission or acquiescence on the part of the Southern States at this perilous hour will enable Black Republicanism to redeem all its nefarious pledges and accomplish all its flagitious ends," Hale concluded.[5]

Alabama's mission to Kentucky ended in failure. Governor Magoffin called the legislature into extra session in response to Hale's letter, but a sharply divided Kentucky refused to follow the path of secession.[6] Yet the importance of this document lay not in what Hale accomplished but in what he said and the way in which he said it. This relatively obscure Alabama politician touched on almost every major point in the secession persuasion, and he did so in language that left no room for doubt or ambiguity. His letter is as passionate, as powerful, and as revealing as any message delivered by any commissioner during those critical weeks in late 1860 and early 1861 when the fate of the Union was hanging in the balance. It is a document that should be required reading for anyone trying to understand the radical mind-set gripping the lower South on the eve of the Civil War.

Hale began by claiming the unquestioned right of any state to secede and by describing the South's previous patience in the face of mounting acts of Northern hostility. In return for their forbearance, however, white Southerners had been dealt a final, intolerable insult. The North had turned the reins of power over to the Black Republican Party and its abolitionist nominee, Abraham Lincoln. Lincoln's election was the crowning indignity because a Republican president was, in Hale's view, a supreme threat to slavery and to the South's racial order.

It was when he moved to describe the consequences of Republican-backed emancipation that Hale revealed what lay at the core of the secession movement in the Deep South. At its heart the drive to destroy the Union fed off the absolute conviction that the abolition of slavery would either plunge the South into a race war or so stain the blood of the white race that it would be contaminated for all time. In the end it came down to this: secede or be prepared to witness the destruction of the race. That destruction might come through "assassinations," it might come through "amalgamation." But the nightmare would come. And no Southern white man, Hale argued, would stand still in the face of such a threat. Who among us, he asked, could remain passive if their inaction meant subjecting their "wives and daughters to pollution and violation to gratify the lust of half-civilized Africans?"

The same dire forecasts that filled the pages of Hale's letter were repeated by other Alabama commissioners as they moved across the South during these weeks. Any doubts about how representative Hale's comments might be quickly disappear when we look at the messages being delivered almost simultaneously in places as distant as Maryland and Missouri.

On December 28 — the day after Hale drafted his communication to Governor Magoffin — Congressman Jabez Lamar Monroe Curry,

Alabama's commissioner to Maryland, was in Annapolis composing a letter to Governor Thomas Hicks.[7]

"The sentiment of the sinfulness of slavery seems to be embedded in the Northern conscience," Curry wrote. "An infidel theory has corrupted the Northern heart." While submission to Lincoln and Republican rule meant "peril and dishonor" for white Southerners, secession meant "deliverance from Abolition domination." Curry closed his letter with a prophecy. "Under an abolition Government the slave-holding states will be placed under a common ban of proscription, and an institution, interwoven in the very frame-work of their social and political being, must perish gradually or speedily with the Government in active hostility to it," he told Hicks. "Instead of the culture and development of the boundless capacities and productive resources of their social system, it is to be assaulted, humbled, dwarfed, degraded, and finally crushed out."[8]

The previous month, before he left Alabama for the opening of Congress, Curry had warned his constituents that "the subjugation of the South to an abolition dynasty" would result in "a saturnalia of blood." Emancipation meant "the abhorrent degradation of social and political equality, the probability of a war of extermination between the races or the necessity of flying the country to avoid the association."[9]

Other Alabama commissioners shared Hale's and Curry's convictions. One day after Curry wrote his letter to Governor Hicks, William Cooper, a prominent lawyer from Tuscumbia and commissioner to Missouri, told that state's legislature that "under the policy of the Republican party, the time would arrive when the scenes of San Domingo and Hayti, with all their attendant horrors, would be enacted in the slaveholding States."[10]

On January 1, 1861, Congressman David Clopton, Alabama's commissioner to Delaware, was in Dover to warn Governor William

Burton that Republicans intended "to circulate insurrectionary documents and disseminate insurrectionary sentiments among a hitherto contented servile population," and that Lincoln's party sought "the establishment of an equality of races in our midst." [11]

On January 3 Judge John Gill Shorter, commissioner to Georgia, told Governor Joseph E. Brown that after March 4 the Lincoln administration "will usurp the machinery of the Federal Government and madly attempt to rule, if not to subjugate, and ruin the South." [12]

Two days later, on January 5, Commissioner James Martin Calhoun was in Austin pleading with Texas governor Sam Houston to support secession. Disunion was the only way to protect the South's white citizens from "utter ruin and degradation," Calhoun wrote. [13]

In his speech to the Virginia General Assembly on January 15, Commissioner Arthur Francis Hopkins, former chief justice of the Alabama Supreme Court, predicted that a federal court system corrupted by Republican "higher law" doctrine would "discharge every slave brought before it . . . , and establish them as free-men and equals in our own land." [14]

It was as if Judge William L. Harris of Mississippi had stopped off in Montgomery back in mid-December on his way to Georgia and held a briefing for Alabama's commissioners. Over and over again the Alabamians described the same nightmare world that Commissioner Harris had painted for the Georgia legislature: a South humbled, abolitionized, degraded, and threatened with destruction by a brutal Republican majority. Emancipation, race war, miscegenation—one apocalyptic vision after another. The death throes of white supremacy would be so horrific that no self-respecting Southerner could fail to rally to the secessionist cause, they argued. Only through disunion could the South preserve the purity and ensure the survival of the white race.

CHAPTER 5

The Mission to Virginia

NO state meant more to the secessionist cause than Virginia. If the state's manpower, wealth, industrial and agricultural resources, and prestige as the cradle of the Founding Fathers and the birthplace of presidents could be placed at the service of the Confederacy, the new government organizing in Montgomery would be dramatically strengthened. If war should come, Virginia's physical assets might be sufficient to tip the scale of battle in favor of the slave South. One thing was certain. If the seven states of the lower South began armed conflict against the Union without the Old Dominion, there could be little doubt as to the ultimate outcome.

The Virginia General Assembly, meeting in regular session early in 1861, passed legislation on January 14 authorizing a state convention. The election of delegates was to take place on February 4, and the convention was to begin in Richmond nine days later. Virginia's fate was still undecided during these weeks. Unionism remained a potent force, particularly in the far western counties, and hope for some sort of sectional compromise persisted across much of the state.[1]

The vote on February 4 clearly showed that a moderate majority would dominate the convention, at least in its initial deliberations. Of the 152 delegates chosen, fewer than 40 were straight-out secessionists.[2] But the summoning of the convention presented the radicals, both inside and outside Virginia, with a forum and an opportunity. Secessionist delegates could keep up a drumbeat for independence while waiting for events (like the crisis building at Fort Sumter) to advance their cause. And secession commissioners could head to the Virginia capital knowing that an all-important audience stood ready to listen to their views.

By the opening of the convention on February 13, three commissioners had arrived in Richmond. Fulton Anderson of Mississippi, Henry Lewis Benning of Georgia, and John Smith Preston of South Carolina presented their credentials and waited for a formal invitation to address the convention.[3] A Unionist delegate from the Valley of Virginia noted wryly that the presence of the commissioners might give the early hours of the convention "something to do, on questions of acceptance of *foreign ambassadors*," but there was never any doubt that the three men would be heard.[4] After consultation with the commissioners, the delegates set February 18 as the date the three visiting dignitaries would speak before the convention.[5]

The day before he was scheduled to give his address, John Smith Preston reported back to South Carolina on his private conversations with a number of convention members. These discussions had not been encouraging, he told South Carolina's newly elected governor, Francis W. Pickens. Those delegates favoring "instant secession" were "very few—perhaps under forty," Preston estimated. "Of the entire Convention I have not found ten men—who contemplated the fact that Virginia has at this moment to choose the Northern or Southern Confederacy," he continued. "All are under the strange delusion that the Southern Confederacy is to be voluntarily dissolved, and the former Union reconstructed." Such wishful thinking on the part of a majority of the delegates was the single most important obstacle standing in the way of the state's secession, Preston believed. It was this conviction—"this illusion of a re-construction"—that Preston had been laboring "day and night" to dispel. "Tomorrow in my address to the Convention I will make this one of my main points—so will the Georgia and perhaps the Mississippi Commissioners," he wrote. Virginians had to be made to face the fact that there would be no turning back on the part of the lower South, no reunion, no "re-construction." Preston closed this long, confidential communication with a prescient observation. "Virginia will not take sides until she is absolutely forced," he predicted.[6]

Preston knew that his words would not move the convention to action, but he also knew that he and his fellow commissioners had to make the best possible case both for secession and, as he told Pickens, for the finality of disunion. In what appears to be an arrangement reached by the commissioners themselves, Fulton Anderson would speak first, Henry L. Benning would follow, and Preston, one of the South's most renowned orators, would give the final address. The convention would assemble at noon on Monday, February 18, to hear them.[7]

A Mississippi acquaintance described Fulton Anderson as "a man of fine talents" and "judicial learning" who "speaks remarkably well."[8] Anderson was a leading member of the bar in Jackson and had had ample opportunity to hone his oratorical skills. But as a longtime member of the Whig Party and a Unionist until deep into the secession crisis, he seemed at first glance an odd choice for the critical mission to Virginia. As late as December 1860, he had run as a Cooperationist candidate for the Mississippi Convention and had lost to a straight-out secessionist. And yet his ultimate conversion to radicalism followed exactly the path Mississippians hoped Virginia would take. Who better to speak to moderate Virginians than a former moderate who had seen the error of his ways?[9]

An "immense crowd" gathered at Mechanics' Institute Hall on Monday to listen to the commissioners.[10] After an opening prayer and a brief explanation that Governor John Letcher was absent due to illness, Commissioner Anderson ascended the platform and began his remarks. He briefly paid homage to Virginia's role "in the first great struggle for independence" and the state's "sacrifices . . . in the cause of the common government," and then he launched into a blistering attack on the Republican Party and all its works. It was an organization "founded upon the idea of unrelenting and eternal hostility to the institution of slavery," he insisted, and its clear purpose was "to take possession of the power of the Government and use it to our destruction." The Lincoln administration aimed at nothing less than "the ultimate extinction of slavery, and the degradation of the Southern people," and he outlined the steps the government would take to achieve these nefarious ends: the exclusion of slavery from the territories, the abolition of slavery in the District of Columbia, the corruption of the federal judiciary, the admission of additional free states into the Union, and the final marshaling of a constitutional majority to sweep the South's peculiar institution into oblivion. The men and women of the South would "become a degraded and a subject class," forced "to bend our necks to the yoke which a false fanaticism had prepared for them."

Virginians did not have to look far for proof of Northern designs, Anderson continued. The purpose of John Brown's raid on Harpers Ferry was "to light up the fires of a servile insurrection, and to give your dwellings to the torch of the incendiary, and your wives and children to the knives of assassins," he said. This "daring outrage on your soil" was "the necessary and logical result of the principles, boldly and recklessly advanced by the sectional party . . . which is now about to be inaugurated into power." And Harpers Ferry was but a foretaste of what Virginians, and indeed all white Southerners, could "expect in the future when the party, whose principles thus give encouragement, aid and comfort to felons and traitors, shall have firmly established its dominion over you."

Anderson explained at some length why the states of the lower South would never return to the Union. "An infidel fanaticism" had so corrupted the Yankee mind that a return to sanity and conservative principles was impossible among "the present generation of the Northern people." They hold Southerners in contempt, he insisted; they believed "that we are a race inferior to them in morality and civilization," and they were committed to "a holy crusade for our benefit in seeking the destruction of that institution which . . . lies at the very foundation of our social and political fabric." The only salvation for the South lay in secession, in "placing our institutions beyond the reach of further hostility." Anderson was attempting to do here exactly what John S. Preston had said the commissioners would do: convince the Virginians that a peaceable return to the status quo ante was out of the question.

It was time to create "a great and powerful Southern Union," Anderson said as he drew his speech to a close. "We invite you to come out from the house of your enemies, and take a proud position in that of your friends and kindred," he added. "Come and be received as an elder brother whose counsels will guide our action and whose leadership we will willingly follow." [11]

Anderson sounded many of the same notes that commissioners had been using across the South in the weeks following Lincoln's election, but his address apparently failed to stir the large audience. A secessionist newspaper in Richmond simply noted that Anderson's words were "listened to with marked attention." [12] Benning and Preston would have to do a better job of persuading the Virginians to calculate the value of the Union.

For Henry L. Benning the sectional crisis of the 1850s represented an opportunity to restart a political career that had met with only limited success up to that point. Benning, a native Georgian, a prominent judge and lawyer, a lifelong Democrat, and a man of considerable wealth (he owned ninety slaves in 1860), always believed that he deserved a better fate at the hands of the voters of Georgia. In 1834 he had graduated first in his class at the University of Georgia, and it was a triumph from which he apparently never recovered. He could not understand why classmates like Howell Cobb and Herschel V. Johnson won victory after victory at the polls while his political aspirations were almost always thwarted. He consistently took a strong Southern rights position in the early 1850s but failed to win a seat in Congress as Georgia, and most of the South, initially rallied behind the Compromise of 1850.

In 1853 when the General Assembly elected the thirty-nine-year-old Benning to a seat on the Georgia Supreme Court, however, he became the youngest man in the state's history to serve on that bench. As a justice he held to an extreme states' rights legal philosophy and argued in a famous case, *Padleford v. Savannah,* that a state supreme court was not bound by decisions of the United States Supreme Court on constitutional questions because the two courts were "co-ordinate and co-equal." He failed to win reelection to the Georgia court in 1859, but on January 2, 1861, Benning's moment finally arrived: in a special election called to choose delegates to a Georgia Convention, he won a seat as a straight-out, immediate secessionist. After Georgia seceded on January 19, the convention chose Benning as Georgia's commissioner to the commonwealth of Virginia.[13]

"What was the reason that induced Georgia to take the step of secession?" Benning asked as he opened his speech to the Virginia delegates. "This reason may be summed up in a single proposition," he answered. "It was a conviction, a deep conviction on the part of

Georgia, that a separation from the North was the only thing that could prevent the abolition of her slavery."

Benning then proceeded to lay out a series of propositions intended to prove that Lincoln's election was a death sentence for the institution of slavery.

First, "the Black Republican party of the North" embraced "a sentiment of hatred to slavery as extreme as hatred can exist."

Second, the Republicans were "in a permanent majority" in the North. "Sir, you cannot overthrow such a party as that," he added. "As well might you attempt to lift a mountain out of its bed and throw it into the sea."

Third, "the North has invariably exerted against slavery, all the power which it had at the time." He cited the abolition of slavery in the Northern states, the fight over the Missouri Compromise and the Wilmot Proviso, and John Brown's raid as proof of this claim.

Benning's final proposition was by far the most interesting. The North was already well along the road to "acquiring the power to abolish slavery." To establish this argument, he went well beyond the usual subjects—new free states carved out of the territories and the passage of a constitutional amendment emancipating the South's slave population. These things would indeed happen, Benning argued. But, he asked, what about slavery in border areas like Delaware and Maryland? "The anti-slavery feeling has got[ten] to be so great at the North that the owners of slave property in these states have a presentiment that it is a doomed institution," he claimed, "and the instincts of self-interest impels them to get rid of that property which is doomed." As a result slavery would be pushed "lower and lower, until it all gets to the Cotton States," Benning maintained. "There is the weight of a continent forcing it down." When the day arrived that the institution was confined to the lower South, "slavery shall be abolished, and if a master refuses to yield to this policy, he shall doubtless be hung for his disobedience." [14]

Up to this point in his address, Benning had taken an approach that would have surprised no one who knew anything about the Georgia commissioner's oratorical style. Benning's speeches were marked "by common sense, cogent, compact reasoning," and "the pure gold of logic," according to a friend who knew him well. "He was not what men generally term an eloquent speaker," this observer noted. [15] Yet eloquence, or something close to it, was certainly called for at this critical moment. Virginia was all-important, and Benning, it seems clear, was determined to make every effort to rise to the occasion. After he finished laying out his point-by-point argument for the inevitability of Republican-led emancipation, Benning abruptly shifted to a much more passionate and emotionally charged appeal.

"If things are allowed to go on as they are, it is certain that slavery is to be abolished except in Georgia and the other cotton States, and . . . ultimately in these States also," Benning insisted. "By the time the North shall have attained the power, the black race will be in a large majority, and then we will have black governors, black legislatures, black juries, black everything"—a comment the audience greeted with "laughter," according to a reporter present. "Is it to be supposed that the white race will stand that?" Benning asked. "It is not a supposable case."

Like other commissioners, Benning saw a nightmarish scenario ahead for the South. War would "break out everywhere like hidden fire from the earth," he predicted, and "a standing army" from the North as well as thousands of Northern "volunteers and Wide-Awakes"—a reference to the Republican marching clubs that had filled the streets of Northern cities during the recent presidential campaign—would descend upon the South to assist the slaves engaged in mortal combat with their masters. The results of this unequal struggle were not in doubt: "We will be overpowered and our men will be compelled to wander like vagabonds all over the earth," he told his audience, "and as for our women, the horrors of their state we cannot contemplate in imagination." This, then, was "the fate which Abolition will bring upon the white race." Benning closed this portion of his speech with a solemn forecast. "We will be completely exterminated," he told the Virginians, "and the land will be left in the possession of the blacks, and then it will go back to a wilderness and become another Africa or St. Domingo."

After spending several minutes sketching a glowing picture of Virginia's commercial and manufacturing prosperity in a new Southern Confederacy, Benning reached the emotional and oratorical climax of his address. "Join the North, and what will become of you?" he asked the delegates. "They will hate you and your institutions as much as they do now, and treat you accordingly," he warned. "Suppose they elevated [Charles] Sumner to the Presidency? Suppose they elevated Fred. Douglas[s], your escaped slave, to the Presidency?" There were "hundreds of thousands at the North who would do this for the purpose of humiliating and insulting the South," he insisted. "What would be your position in such an event?" Benning had his own clear and unequivocal answer to this question: "I say give me pestilence and famine sooner than that."

At the conclusion of his lengthy speech, Benning assured the Richmond audience that disunion was final. To emphasize this point, he turned dramatically to John Janney, the president of the convention, and handed him a copy of Georgia's Ordinance of Secession. "Above all, we have a cause—the cause of honor, and liberty, and property, and self-preservation," Benning told the Virginians. "Sir, in such a cause, cowards will become men, men heroes, and heroes gods." [16]

By the time Benning had finished speaking, the hour had grown late, and the delegates decided to postpone Preston's speech until noon on Tuesday, February 19.[17] The convention, and the public, would have to wait one more day to hear one of the South's premier orators.

Reaction to the first two speeches depended largely on the political stance of the listener. Robert Y. Conrad, a moderate Unionist delegate from Winchester, was singularly unimpressed. While the addresses were being delivered, he wrote a note to his wife telling her that the convention was "just now engaged in listening to the harangues of the ambassadors from the cotton states."[18] And convention president John Janney, another moderate Unionist, seems to have shared Conrad's assessment. "Today we have heard Mr. Anderson of Mississippi and Mr. Benning of Georgia and *certainly* there is no body on our side either killed or wounded or frightened," Janney wrote his wife that evening. "Tomorrow we are to hear Mr. Preston of South Carolina and then I hope we shall be at the end of the ambassadors," he added.[19]

The local secessionist press saw some merit in the addresses of that first day, but even here the initial reaction was muted. "Able speeches were delivered by Hon. Fulton Anderson of Mississippi, and Hon. Henry L. Benning of Georgia," the *Richmond Daily Dispatch* reported on February 19. It was clear that the radicals were counting heavily on John S. Preston. If a speaker of his stature could not move a Virginia audience on the question of secession, who indeed could?

John Smith Preston, like so many of the commissioners, was a native of the state to which he was sent. Born in 1809 into a distinguished Virginia family, Preston had studied at Hampden-Sydney College, the University of Virginia, and Harvard before setting up a legal practice at Abingdon in southwestern Virginia. After ten years as a small-town lawyer, however, Preston set his sights on a more lucrative career. He was assisted in this process by his ties to one of South Carolina's wealthiest families. In 1830 he had married Caroline Martha Hampton, the daughter of General Wade Hampton Sr. In 1840 Preston and his family moved south, first to South Carolina and shortly thereafter to Louisiana, where Preston made a fortune as a sugar planter.

After he and his family returned to South Carolina in 1848, Preston established himself as a patron of the arts and began building a reputation as a public speaker. He served in the South Carolina senate from 1848 to 1856 and emerged there as an ardent defender of Southern rights. But in 1856 he abandoned his political career and took his family to live in Europe. His children were educated there, and Preston gave free rein to one of his principal passions—art collecting.

The Prestons returned to South Carolina in 1860 in time for John to play an important role in the crisis gripping his adopted state. In November he helped launch the "Minute Men" of Columbia, a pro-secessionist organization, and the following month he was elected to the South Carolina Convention. This body chose Preston as the state's commissioner to Virginia as soon as word reached Charleston that the Virginians were organizing a state convention.[20]

According to a report in the *Columbia South Carolinian,* some members of the Charleston convention originally had wanted to send Preston to some other state, but this suggestion had been greeted with cries of "No, no, let us reserve him for Virginia."[21] Much was expected of this man and his oratory.

One Richmond observer noted that a "throng more dense than yesterday" filled Mechanics' Institute Hall on February 19 in anticipation of Preston's appearance.[22] Following the customary opening prayer, President Janney introduced the commissioner from South Carolina, and Preston came forward to begin the most important speech of his career.

Preston began by assuring his audience that he would waste no time arguing the constitutionality of secession. South Carolina had surrendered none of its sovereignty when it ratified the Constitution, and therefore the state's Ordinance of Secession was nothing more than the termination of a voluntary compact. His primary purpose, he informed the crowded chamber, was "to lay before you the causes which induced the State of South Carolina to withdraw from the Union."

"For fully thirty years or more, the people of the Northern States have assailed the institution of African slavery," Preston charged. During these three decades "large masses of their people" embraced "the most fearful" path to emancipation: "the subject race . . . rising and murdering their masters." Virginians need look no farther than their own northern border for the most recent manifestation of Yankee fanaticism. John Brown and his followers had brazenly "proclaimed the intention of abolishing slavery by the annihilation of the slaveholders." There could be no doubt, he continued, "that the conflict between slavery and non-slavery is a conflict for life and death." Preston interpreted Lincoln's election as a "decree" of "annihilation" for the white people of the South. South Carolina had a God-given right to protect itself against this "mad rage of fanaticism," and it had done so.

Preston went to considerable lengths to defend his state against charges of "rash precipitancy." Nonsense, he said. South Carolina had suffered abuse after abuse for years without responding. "As long as it was a merely silly fanaticism or a prurient philanthropy that proposed our destruction, we scarcely complained," he insisted. "Even when . . . unjust, partial and oppressive taxation was grinding us into the very dust of poverty . . . we bore that happily." Now, however, the "fermenting millions" of the North had "seized the Constitution . . . and distorted it into an instrument of our instant ruin." Hesitation under these circumstances "seems to us not only base cowardice, but absolute fatuity," he added, and the crowd responded with a burst of applause.

The emotional climax of Preston's address came toward the end. "Gentlemen of Virginia," he called. The people of the South "are not canting fanatics, festering in the licentiousness of abolition and amalgamation; their liberty is not a painted strumpet, straggling through the streets; nor does their truth need to baptize itself in pools of blood." No, he cried, Southerners "are a calm, grave, deliberate and religious people, the holders of the most majestic civilization and the inheritors, by right, of the fairest estate of liberty." And South Carolina was no longer standing alone in defense of the sacred soil of the South. Florida, Alabama, Georgia, Mississippi, Louisiana, "and now young Texas" had formed a "majestic column of confederated sovereignties." Would Virginia join them? Would the sons of the Old Dominion stand idle at this moment of supreme peril? "I . . . told my countrymen, that before the spring grass grows long enough to weave one chaplet of victory, they will hear the sound as of the tramp of a mighty host of men, and they will see floating before that host the banner whose whole history is one blaze of glory, and not one blot of shame," Preston intoned. "And on that banner will be written the unsullied name of Virginia."

The audience packed into Mechanics' Institute Hall interrupted Preston with wave after wave of applause during this rhetorical flight. But he was not quite finished. As he had written Governor Pickens two days earlier, he had to convince the Virginians that secession was irreversible, that, in Preston's words, "there can never again be a reconstruction of the late Federal Union."

To demonstrate this point Preston put forward an argument similar to the one Commissioner Leonidas Spratt had used in speaking to the Florida Convention. The North and the South constituted two separate, distinct, and antagonistic civilizations, Preston insisted, and nothing could "amalgamate a people whose severance is proclaimed by the most rigid requisitions of universal necessity." The critical difference was the most obvious one. "The South cannot exist without African slavery," he said. "None but an equal race can labor at the North; none but a subject race will labor at the South." There were other "repellant diversities" that made "the political union . . . an unnatural and monstrous one," but slavery, and race, formed the heart of the matter.

Preston ended his address with a sharp-edged appeal to Virginian pride. He asked whether the delegates would, "like the trembling Egyptian, . . . skulk for protection beneath the crumbling fragments of an ancient greatness . . . or whether you will step forth . . . and keep the ancient glory of your name." Nothing less than the survival of the South was at stake, he warned as he drew his oration to a close.[23]

"On all hands we hear one unqualified and enthusiastic expression of praise and admiration of the great address of the Commissioner of South Carolina," noted the *Richmond Daily Dispatch* on February 21. "Patriotism, passion, power, poetry, were all combined in this magnificent effort," the editorial continued. "At one time the whole audience was in tears."

Another Richmonder who heard the speech called it "a splendid oration" with "many bursts of real eloquence, electrifying his audience." This listener described Preston as a "master of three different manners—the calm, slow, didactic style—then the impetuous and vehement—and lastly the solemn and pathetic." The huge crowd responded by "bursting out repeatedly in uncontrolled applause."[24]

The most fascinating reaction to the speeches of the three commissioners came on February 22, three days after Preston's performance. In a moment of supreme, albeit unintended, irony, the editor of the *Daily Dispatch* suggested that Richmond's most spacious indoor meeting facility should be obtained so that the commissioners could repeat their addresses for an even greater audience; that building, the editor pointed out, was "the African Church," home of Richmond's largest black congregation.

Preston had told Governor Pickens before he gave his speech that Virginia would "not take sides until she is absolutely forced," and this prediction proved remarkably accurate. He may have moved his audience to tears, but he did not move Virginia into the Confederate column. Lewis E. Harvie, a leading secessionist delegate and president of the Richmond and Danville Railroad, telegraphed Preston on March 6 that "we are still in a minority in Convention—waiting for the force of events." [25]

Those events came in April with the firing on Fort Sumter and Lincoln's call for troops. Only then did the Virginia Convention become what Preston, Henry Benning, and Fulton Anderson had tried to make it become—a force for disunion and an agent of the state's secession.

Conclusion:
Apostles of Disunion,
Apostles of Racism

J OHN Smith Preston spent the war years in uniform. After serving in a number of different staff positions in the army, he found a home in the Confederate Bureau of Conscription. He took over that agency in 1863, was promoted to the rank of brigadier general in 1864, and headed the Conscript Bureau until the South went down to defeat. Preston lived for a time in England after the war, but in 1868 he went back to South Carolina.[1] His reputation as an orator still intact, Preston was invited to return to his native state in 1868 to address the Washington and Jefferson Societies of the University of Virginia. On June 30 of that year, Preston spoke in Charlottesville to the young Virginians.

Much of his address was an eloquent tribute to the Founding Fathers and their principal handiwork—the Revolution, the state constitutions, and the Constitution of the United States. Through their efforts "your fathers achieved that liberty which comes of a free government, founded on justice, order and peace," Preston said. In order to preserve the principles and the constitutional forms established by the Revolutionary generation, "you, the immediate offspring of the founders, went forth to that death grapple which has prevailed against you," he continued. It was the North, "the victors," who rejected "the principles," destroyed "the forms," and defeated "the promised destiny of America," Preston charged. "The Constitution you fought for"—the Confederate Constitution—"embodied every principle of the Constitution of the United States, and guaranteed the free Constitution of Virginia. It did not omit one essential for liberty and the public welfare," he claimed. The Confederacy was in ashes, however, and so was true constitutional liberty. "That liberty was lost, and now the loud hosanna is shouted over land and sea—'Liberty may be dead, but the Union is preserved. Glory, glory, glory to Massachusetts and her Hessian and Milesian mercenaries,'" Preston declaimed. Yet all was not lost. Even though "cruel, bloody, remorseless tyrants may rule at Fort Sumter and at Richmond . . . they cannot crush that immortal hope, which rises from the blood soaked earth of Virginia," Preston believed. "I see the sacred image of regenerate Virginia, and cry aloud, in the hearing of a God of Right, and in the hearing of all the nations of the earth—ALL HAIL OUR MOTHER."[2]

Passionate, unregenerate, unapologetic, unreconstructed—all these and more apply to Preston's remarks on this occasion. But so do words like "conveniently forgetful," "strongly revisionist," and "purposely misleading." Nowhere to be found are references to many of the arguments and descriptions he had used over and over again before the Virginia Convention in February 1861—things like "the subject race . . . rising and murdering their masters" or "the conflict between slavery and non-slavery is a conflict for life and death," or his insistence that "the South cannot exist without African slavery," or his portrait of the "fermenting millions" of the North as "canting, fanatics, festering in the licentiousness of abolition and amalgamation." All this was swept aside as Preston sought to paint the Civil War as a mighty struggle over differing concepts of constitutional liberty. Like Jefferson Davis and Alexander H. Stephens in their postwar writings, Preston was trying to reframe the causes of the conflict in terms that would be much more favorable to the South.

Preston was not the only former secession commissioner to launch such an effort after the war. Jabez L. M. Curry, who had served as Alabama's commissioner to Maryland in December 1860, became a leading figure in the drive to improve primary and secondary education in the postwar South. As agent for both the Peabody and Slater Funds and as supervising director of the Southern Education Board, Curry worked tirelessly to establish public schools and teacher training for both races in the states of the former Confederacy. Curry also worked diligently to justify the Lost Cause of the Confederacy. In his *Civil History of the Government of the Confederate States, with Some Personal Reminiscences,* published in Richmond in 1901, Curry offered an analysis of the coming of the war that closely paralleled the argument used by John S. Preston in 1868. "The object in quitting the Union was not to destroy, but to save the principles of the Constitution," Curry wrote. "The Southern States from the beginning of the government had striven to keep it within the orbit prescribed by the Constitution and failed."[3] The Curry of 1901 would hardly have recognized the Curry of 1860, who told the governor of Maryland that secession meant "deliverance from Abolition domination," and who predicted that under Republican rule the South's slave-based social system would "be assaulted, humbled, dwarfed, degraded, and finally crushed out."

In 1860 and 1861 Preston, Curry, and the other commissioners had seen a horrific future facing their region within the confines of Abraham Lincoln's Union. When they used words like "submission" and "degradation," when they referred to "final subjugation" and "annihilation," they were not talking about constitutional differences or political arguments. They were talking about the dawning of an abominable new world in the South, a world created by the Republican destruction of the institution of slavery.

The secession commissioners knew what this new and hateful

world would look like. Over and over again they called up three stark images that, taken together, constituted the white South's worst nightmare.

The first threat was the looming specter of racial equality. The commissioners insisted almost to a man that Republican ascendancy in Washington placed white supremacy in the South in mortal peril. Mississippi commissioner William L. Harris made this point clearly and unambiguously in his speech to the Georgia legislature in December 1860. "Our fathers made this a government for the white man," Harris told the Georgians, "rejecting the negro, as an ignorant, inferior, barbarian race, incapable of self-government, and not, therefore, entitled to be associated with the white man upon terms of civil, political, or social equality." But the Republicans intended "to overturn and strike down this great feature of our Union . . . and to substitute in its stead their new theory of the universal equality of the black and white races." Alabama's commissioners to North Carolina, Isham W. Garrott and Robert H. Smith, predicted that the white children of their state would "be compelled to flee from the land of their birth, and from the slaves their parents have toiled to acquire as an inheritance for them, or to submit to the degradation of being reduced to an equality with them, and all its attendant horrors." South Carolina's John McQueen warned the Texas Convention that Lincoln and the Republicans were bent upon "the abolition of slavery upon this continent and the elevation of our own slaves to an equality with ourselves and our children." And so it went, as commissioner after commissioner—Leonidas Spratt of South Carolina, David Clopton and Arthur F. Hopkins of Alabama, Henry L. Benning of Georgia—hammered home this same point.

The impending imposition of racial equality informed the speeches of other commissioners as well. Thomas J. Wharton, Mississippi's attorney general and that state's commissioner to Tennessee, said in Nashville on January 8, 1861, that the Republican Party would, "at no distant day, inaugurate the reign of equality of all races and colors, and the universality of the elective franchise."⁴ Commissioner Samuel L. Hall of Georgia told the North Carolina legislature on February 13, 1861, that only a people "dead to all sense of virtue and dignity" would embrace the Republican doctrine of "the social and political equality of the black and white races."⁵ Another Georgia commissioner, Luther J. Glenn of Atlanta, made the same point to the Missouri legislature on March 2, 1861. The Republican platform, press, and principal spokesmen had made their "purposes, objects, and motives" crystal clear, Glenn insisted: "hostility to the South, the extinction of slavery, and the ultimate elevation of the negro to civil, political and social equality with the white man." These reasons and these reasons alone had prompted his state "to dissolve her connexion with the General Government," Glenn insisted.⁶

The second element in the commissioners' prophecy was the prospect of a race war. Mississippi commissioner Alexander H. Handy raised this threat in his Baltimore speech in December 1860—Republican agents infiltrating the South "to excite the slave to cut the throat of his master." Alabamians Garrott and Smith told their Raleigh audience that Republican policies would force the South either to abandon slavery "or be doomed to a servile war." William Cooper, Alabama's commissioner to Missouri, delivered a similar message in Jefferson City. "Under the policy of the Republican party, the time would arrive when the scenes of San Domingo and Hayti, with all their attendant horrors, would be enacted in the slaveholding States," he told the Missourians. David Clopton of Alabama wrote the governor of Delaware that Republican ascendancy "endangers instead of insuring domestic tranquility by the possession of channels through which to circulate insurrectionary documents and disseminate insurrectionary sentiments among a hitherto contented servile population." Wharton of Mississippi told the Tennessee legislature that Southerners "will not, cannot surrender our institutions," and that Republican attempts to subvert slavery "will drench the country in blood, and extirpate one or other of the races."[7] In their speeches to the Virginia Convention, Fulton Anderson, Henry L. Benning, and John S. Preston all forecast a Republican-inspired race war that would, as Benning put it, "break out everywhere like hidden fire from the earth."

The third prospect in the commissioners' doomsday vision was, in many ways, the most dire: racial amalgamation. Judge Harris of Mississippi sounded this note in Georgia in December 1860 when he spoke of Republican insistence on "equality in the rights of matrimony." Other commissioners repeated this warning in the weeks that followed. In Virginia, Henry Benning insisted that under Republican-led abolition "our women" would suffer "horrors . . . we cannot contemplate in imagination." There was not an adult present who could not imagine exactly what Benning was talking about. Leroy Pope Walker, Alabama's commissioner to Tennessee and subsequently the first Confederate secretary of war, predicted that in the absence of secession all would be lost—first, "our property," and "then our liberties," and finally the South's greatest treasure, "the sacred purity of our daughters."[8]

No commissioner articulated the racial fears of the secessionists better, or more graphically, than Alabama's Stephen F. Hale. When he wrote of a South facing "amalgamation or extermination," when he referred to "all the horrors of a San Domingo servile insurrection," when he described every white Southerner "degraded to a position of equality with free negroes," when he foresaw the "sons and daughters" of the South "associating with free negroes upon terms of political and social equality," when he spoke of the Lincoln administration consigning the citizens of the South "to assassinations and her wives and daughters to pollution and violation to gratify the lust of half-civilized Africans," he was giving voice to the night terrors of the secessionist South. States' rights, historic political abuses, territorial questions, economic differences, constitutional arguments—all these and more paled into insignificance when placed alongside this vision of the South's future under Republican domination.

The choice was absolutely clear. The slave states could secede and establish their independence, or they could submit to "Black Republican" rule with its inevitable consequences: Armageddon or amalgamation. Whites forced to endure racial equality, race war, a staining of the blood—who could tolerate such things?

The commissioners sent out to spread the secessionist gospel in late 1860 and early 1861 clearly believed that the racial fate of their region was hanging in the balance in the wake of Lincoln's election. Only through disunion could the South be saved from the disastrous effects of Republican principles and Republican malevolence. Hesitation, submission—any course other than immediate secession—would place both slavery and white supremacy on the road to certain extinction. The commissioners were arguing that disunion, even if it meant risking war, was the only way to save the white race.

Did these men really believe these things? Did they honestly think that secession was necessary in order to stay the frenzied hand of the Republican abolitionist, preserve racial purity and racial supremacy, and save their women and children from rape and slaughter at the hands of "half-civilized Africans"? They made these statements, and used the appropriate code words, too many times in too many places with too much fervor and raw emotion to leave much room for doubt. They knew these things in the marrow of their bones, and they destroyed a political union because of what they believed and what they foresaw.

But, we might ask, could they not see the illogicality, indeed the absurdity, of their insistence that Lincoln's election meant that the white South faced the sure prospect of either massive miscegenation or a race war to the finish? They seem to have been totally untroubled by logical inconsistencies of this sort. Indeed, the capacity for compartmentalization among this generation of white Southerners appears to have been practically boundless. How else can we explain Judge William L. Harris's comments before the Mississippi State Agricultural Society in November 1858? "It has been said by an eminent statesman," Harris observed on this occasion, "'that nothing can advance the mass of society in prosperity and happiness, nothing can uphold the substantial interest and steadily improve the general condition and character of the whole, but this one thing—compensating rewards for labor.'"[9] It apparently never occurred to Harris that this observation might apply to the hundreds of thousands of slaves working in Mississippi in 1858 as well as to the white farmers and mechanics of his adopted state. His mind could not even comprehend the possibility that slaves, too, were human beings who, if given the opportunity, might well respond to "compensating rewards" for their labor.

In setting out to explain secession to their fellow Southerners, the commissioners have explained a very great deal to us as well. By illuminating so clearly the racial content of the secession persuasion, the commissioners would seem to have laid to rest, once and for all, any notion that slavery had nothing to do with the coming of the Civil War. To put it quite simply, slavery and race were absolutely critical elements in the coming of the war. Neo-Confederate groups may have "a problem" with this interpretation, as the leader of the Virginia Heritage Preservation Association put it. But these defenders of the Lost Cause need only read the speeches and letters of the secession commissioners to learn what was really driving the Deep South to the brink of war in 1860–61.

Afterword
Apostles of Disunion
Fifteen Years Later

I
t was a day I never thought I would see in this country.

On the evening of November 4, 2008, I was glued to the television set as the presidential election returns came flashing across the screen—state after state tipping into the Democratic column, even bastions of the Old Confederacy like Virginia and North Carolina—and it soon became clear that for the first time in our race-haunted, frequently blood-drenched history, something close to the impossible was actually happening: the voters of the United States of America had elevated an African American man to the highest office in our land.

I watched as Barack Obama, accompanied by his wife, Michelle, and their two young daughters, came out on a stage erected in Grant Park in Chicago to address an enormous crowd—some estimates put the number of people in attendance at 250,000.[1] As the president-elect spoke, the television cameras swung frequently to show the faces of his listeners—Caucasian, African American, Asian American, Latino/Latina, every race and nationality seemed to be represented in that ecstatic crowd—and I suddenly realized that tears were rolling down my face. It took me a moment, but I quickly understood what was happening. I was literally shedding tears of joy. I thought that I was watching my country at the dawn of a new era, a time of racial reconciliation when we, collectively, all of us, could consign the sordid, racist, and bigoted elements of our past to their much-deserved place in the dustbin of history. We could start saying "racism was," not "racism is."

It seemed too good to be true.

And, of course, it was. Our long racial nightmare was far from over. There was a continuing, and patently phony, race-based "birther" controversy over President Obama's supposedly Kenyan birthplace. The rise of an overwhelmingly white "Tea Party" movement on the right wing of American politics was marked by rallies where members waved the Confederate battle flag and carried signs bearing crude racial caricatures of the president. In an unprecedented display of open contempt, Representative Joe Wilson of South Carolina shouted, "You lie!" at the president as he addressed a joint session of Congress in 2009. The Southern Poverty Law Center reported an explosive growth in the number of white supremacist hate groups across the country.[2]

And then came the killings of African Americans (and only the most prominent cases made the national news): Trayvon Martin in Sanford, Florida, in 2012; Eric Garner in Staten Island, New York, Michael Brown in Ferguson, Missouri, and Tamir Rice in Cleveland, Ohio, in 2014; Walter Scott in North Charleston, South Carolina, in 2015. The climax of this wave of bloodletting also occurred in South Carolina, in the city of Charleston, on the night of June 17, 2015.

That evening the Bible study group at the Emanuel African Methodist Episcopal Church in downtown Charleston was joined by a twenty-one-year-old white South Carolinian named Dylann Storm Roof. He was welcomed, sat for an hour, and then, shortly after 9:00 PM, opened fire on the black church members. A survivor of the shooting reported that Roof said, as he was carrying out the murder of nine African American men and women, "I have to do it. You rape our women and you're taking over our country, and you have to go." Roof's hope and expectation was that these killings would spark a race war in the United States. He had already posted on the web a racist manifesto and photographs of himself, one of which showed him posing with a firearm in one hand and a small Confederate battle flag in the other.[3]

The linking of the racial murders at Emanuel A.M.E. Church with the battle flag of the Confederacy triggered a fierce debate over Confederate symbolism in South Carolina and elsewhere across the South. Governor Nikki Haley of South Carolina called for the removal of the Confederate flag from the grounds of the State Capitol in Columbia, and the legislature, after a lengthy and contentious debate, agreed. The Confederate flag was lowered on July 10, 2015, less than a month after the murder of the nine members of the Bible study group at Emanuel Church.[4]

These killings in multiple locations across the United States gave added urgency to a project I was working on during these years: an account of my growing up on the white side of the color line in the Jim Crow South. That story has now been published and carries the title *The Making of a Racist: A Southerner Reflects on Family, History, and the Slave Trade.*[5]

I had come to this autobiographical undertaking by a rather circuitous route. After the publication of *Apostles of Disunion* in 2001, I had decided to embark on a study I had tentatively titled "Voices from the Slave South." The "voices" came in the form of some truly remarkable and uniquely powerful documents I had turned up doing archival research over a number of years—documents that had stopped me dead in my tracks the first time I read them. I had singled out eight or nine items for consideration, and my plan was to write a chapter on each document and then try to pull everything together at the end. My concluding chapter would consist of my take on the impact of slavery on the society and culture of the antebellum South.

During my research for this project, I found myself coming back over and over again to a single document, one that had haunted me since the first time I saw it: a price list issued in August 1860 by the slave-trading firm of Betts & Gregory, Auctioneers, of Richmond, Virginia. This one-page broadside listed a range of prices for various categories of men and women ("Extra," "No. 1," "Second rate or Ordinary"), and it priced "Boys" and "Girls" by height, beginning at "4 feet high" and going up by three-inch increments to "5 feet high." The rare book librarian at the institution where I teach, Williams College, had acquired this document in 1999, and he called me over to the library to take a look at it.

I had a highly emotional, gut-wrenching reaction to it the first time I held this price list in my hands and read it. There, on a single page, was the essence of the slave system of the Old South: human be-ings as property, human chattel in the eyes of the law—men, women, boys, and girls transformed into commodities and offered for sale to the highest bidder.[6] How had we white southerners come to this, I asked myself. How could we not see what we were doing back then, treating human beings as livestock, buying them, selling them, tearing families apart, extracting labor from them—millions of them—by force? And it came to me that I had been doing something of the same thing as a boy growing up in the South in the 1940s and '50s. The racial segregation I had been looking in the face every day was not slavery, but, still, wasn't the process of "not seeing" pretty much the same? How had that happened? How had I grown up so blind to the injustice and humiliation that the Jim Crow system inflicted on black men, women, and children every day? Segregation was right there in front of me, omnipresent, every day, and I did not see it.

So I decided to try to answer that question. I would shift my sights from multiple "voices from the slave South" to a new project, one in which I would attempt a fusion of autobiography and history. I would try to combine the "voice" of my own southern upbringing with a single documentary "voice" from the antebellum South. I would start with my own story, and then, using whatever skills I might possess as a historian, I would transition to an examination of the world that lay behind that Betts & Gregory price list. I would use that document as my bridge to a study of the worst of the worst of the Old South, the interstate slave trade. By reading the correspondence of the Richmond slave traders and their clients, maybe I could get inside the mindset of the men who generated that 1860 document. If I could understand their blindness, maybe I could understand my own.

Reading the letters sent to and from Richmond's slave dealers and turning over the pages of their business ledgers was a sobering and depressing exercise. But in doing so, I became more fully aware of something I had noted in *Apostles of Disunion* but which I now believed deserved more emphasis than I had originally given to it.

I had traced an economic line of argument running through several of the secession commissioners' speeches and public letters. To cite one example, Stephen Fowler Hale of Alabama had referred to "African slavery" as "this gigantic interest" when he drafted his December 1860 letter to the governor of Kentucky. He had gone on to say that it had not only become "one of the fixed domestic institutions of the Southern States"; it also "constitutes the most valuable species of their property, worth, according to recent estimates, not less than $4,000,000,000." Slavery, Hale insisted, was the foundation "upon which rests the prosperity and wealth of most of these States."[7]

I had noted Hale's comments on the South's economic stake in slavery in my discussion of his long letter and had provided the full text of this document in an appendix. But now I wondered if I had

failed to give adequate attention to something of genuine importance here. And if I had missed something of significance in Hale's
communication, a document as important as any piece of evidence I
examined in my book, maybe I had done the same thing in my analysis of some of the other messages those "apostles of disunion" were
carrying across the South in late 1860 and early 1861.

In addition to this emphasis on slavery and Southern prosperity,
some commissioners had singled out the slave trade itself for specific
comment. This trade, when it was raised, often contained two di-
mensions, one foreign and the other domestic. Both were discussed
when I reported on the speech given by Isham W. Garrott and Robert Hardy Smith of Alabama when they addressed a joint session of
the North Carolina legislature on December 20, 1860. "The non-
slaveholding States . . . are charging upon us a design to reopen the
African slave trade," I had quoted them as saying. "The charge is a
slander upon our people, and a reflection upon their intelligence."
Deep South buyers, they insisted, "will look, as heretofore, to the
redundant slave population of the more Northern of their associated
sister States of the South for such additions to their negroes as their
wants may require."[8]

These references—to the enormous value of slave property and to
the vital role slavery played in generating Southern economic prosperity, as well as Garrott's and Smith's insistence that the human
commerce linking the upper and lower South would remain intact—
now resonated with me in a new way. They offered corroboration
for something I had found in my examination of the Richmond
slave dealers: the domestic slave trade was a profit-sharing economic
engine of enormous magnitude, carrying much-needed forced labor
to the cotton and sugar fields of the Deep South and sending much-
needed income to the slave-exporting states to the north. Again,
could this theme of Garrott's and Smith's address, like the economic

references in Hale's letter, be found in the messages of other commissioners as well?

In both cases, the answer turned out to be yes.

As I systematically reread the commissioners' speeches and public letters, it became clear that these economic themes formed a significant undercurrent in their case for secession.

"Appeals have been made to your fears—you have been urged to resist this natural and homogenious [*sic*] alliance [with the Confederacy] for the reason that it was the design of the cotton States to re-open the foreign slave trade," Samuel Hall, commissioner from Georgia, told a joint session of the North Carolina legislature on the evening of February 13, 1861. "No considerable portion of our people have ever favored the policy of reviving it," he went on, and the new Confederate Constitution contained a specific clause prohibiting the African trade. "Go on, and continue to raise the supply of labor, and we will provide for our wants in your market," he assured the North Carolinians, using language almost identical to that employed by Garrott and Smith in their December 1860 address to the same body. And the South should never forget that Cotton is King, Commissioner Hall added. "We have that upon which the stability of every throne in Europe rests, and upon which our own prosperity depends," he intoned as he drew his speech to a dramatic close; "the not distant future is radiant with prosperity and renown. Glory awaits us—power and freedom are within our grasp."[9]

Hall's message was clear: glory, power, freedom (for whites only), prosperity, slavery, and the domestic slave trade, all ready to emerge triumphant, together, joined at the hip, as secession carried the day across the length and breadth of the South.

There was one catch to all of this, however. As former Alabama commissioner to North Carolina Robert Hardy Smith told an audience in Mobile on March 30, 1861, the newly drafted Confederate

Constitution also contained a clause declaring that "Congress shall . . . have power to prohibit the introduction of slaves from any State not a member of, or Territory not belonging to, this Confederacy." Smith knew whereof he spoke; he was fresh from having held a seat in the Constitutional Convention that had met in Montgomery earlier that same month. So listen up, Virginia, Maryland, Kentucky, North Carolina, and all you other slave-exporting states, Smith was warning. There is a powerful stick out there as well as the alluring carrot of an uninterrupted domestic slave trade. "I trust it may not be necessary to exercise this power, because I hope to see [all] the Southern States of the United States joined in Government with us," he continued; but this constitutional power "was essential" and would be used if the states of the upper South refused to secede and instead chose "to remain a fringe upon the skirts of New England abolition."[10]

Maryland received dire warnings about the future of its domestic slave trade from two Deep South commissioners.

Alabama's J. L. M. Curry told Governor Thomas Hicks on December 28, 1860, that the inauguration of Abraham Lincoln would mark the end of Maryland's lucrative coastal shipments of slave property to the lower South. "Now, the opinion of nearly every Republican is, that the slave of a citizen of Maryland," even accompanied by his master, "on a vessel sailing from Baltimore to Mobile, is as free as his master . . . as soon as a vessel has reached a marine league beyond the shores of a State, and is outside the jurisdiction of State laws." Alabama was "determined that her slave population, not . . . be increased by importations from Africa," Curry went on, but should Maryland "refuse union with the seceding States," she would "be deprived of an outlet for surplus slaves."[11]

Much the same message was conveyed by Mississippi commissioner Alexander Hamilton Handy. Speaking in Princess Anne County on January 1, 1861, he warned his Maryland audience that once the "wicked and profligate" Black Republicans were in power, they would not hesitate to destroy the South's slave system. "The slave-trade between the States is to be abolished," he predicted, "thereby preventing the exportation of slaves from the Old Southern States [like you, Maryland], until their increase shall become an evil, and compel their emancipation, and thus abolitionize those States."[12]

Not surprisingly, the three Deep South commissioners sent to Virginia also commented on the link between slavery and Southern prosperity, and two of these men addressed the slave trade issue directly.

John Smith Preston argued that the agricultural commodities produced by "slave labor" had always fueled American trade and that in his adopted state of South Carolina, with a population of "300,000 whites and 400,000 slaves," he and his fellow "whites depend on their slaves for their order of civilization and their existence."[13]

Fulton Anderson of Mississippi expressed similar views. The "institution of slavery," he insisted, was the foundation "upon which rests not only the whole wealth of the Southern people, but their very social and political existence." And the Lincoln administration, Anderson warned, would quickly move "to abolish the internal slave trade between the States."[14]

It was Henry Lewis Benning, however, who argued the economic case for secession most fully. After laying out his apocalyptic vision of life under Abraham Lincoln's Union—the end of white supremacy, race war, amalgamation—the commissioner from Georgia turned to describe the golden future that awaited Virginians if they cast their lot with the Confederacy. The commonwealth would become the breadbasket and the industrial heartland of the new Southern republic, he predicted. "Georgia and the other cotton States produce four millions of bales of cotton annually," he noted. "Every one of these bales is worth $50," and the entire "crop, therefore, is worth

$200,000,000." He was confident that the South's slave labor force would increase that 1860 crop of four million bales to six million bales by 1870, and nine million bales by 1890, "and so on" into the twentieth century. Sugar, rice, naval stores, lumber, and "various other articles" would add another $30,000,000 to the South's current productivity and bring the 1860 total "to $230,000,000, with a prospect of vast increase."

How would the Deep South spend this fortune? They would purchase "manufactured goods, iron, cotton and woolen manufactures, ready-made clothing . . . flour, and wheat, and bacon, and pork, and mules, and," most tellingly, "negroes," Benning promised. "Now, I say, why will not Virginia furnish us these goods?" Why not, indeed.

"We offer you riches, and peace, and brotherhood, and glory, and length of days," he continued. "Why, then, will you not come with us? What objections can you have?"

The Georgia commissioner raised one possible objection. "That the African slave trade will be opened?" There was "no danger of that." The Confederate Constitution has specifically closed off that possibility. "Above all, our highest interest is opposed to the reopening of that trade, for were it once reopened, were the barriers once broken down, such a mighty current would rush in from Africa, that our white race would be overwhelmed in the vast black pool."

The domestic slave trade—the trade that really mattered to Virginians—was a more complex matter, however. Benning readily acknowledged the presence of that clause in the Confederate Constitution that gave the new government the power to interdict the interstate trade from states that refused to join the new Confederacy. Was this really a threat aimed at Virginia and the other slave-exporting states of the upper South? "I deny that there is any such threat in this clause," Benning insisted. "Its object was not to threaten you, but to save ourselves." It was in the interest of the Deep South "to keep you a slave State as long as possible," and clearly "the best way to do that would be to prevent your citizens from selling their slaves to ours."

Would such a "threat" (or "non-threat") be carried out? Would Virginia's citizens be barred "from selling their slaves to ours?" Benning's answer undoubtedly sent a chill down the spines of many in his Richmond audience: "I have no doubt, that they would be prevented from doing so."

So there it was. An unambiguous statement that unless the states of the upper South seceded, their lucrative human traffic with the states of the new Confederacy would grind to a halt.

And the fact that Benning held his detailed discussion of Virginia's access to the booming Deep South market for slaves until the close of his address was certainly no accident. Almost immediately after these remarks, he asked a final question: "What objection, then, can you have to joining us and going with your interest, in preference to joining the North and going against your interest? You can have none, as far as I can see. Why, then, will you not join us?"

All that was left for him to do at this point in his lengthy speech was to reference the cause of the South, "the cause of honor, and liberty, and property, and self-preservation," and to insist, "in such a cause, cowards will become men, men heroes, and heroes gods."[15]

I had no idea when I began my investigation of Richmond's slave traders of the monetary value of their business. I knew that one 1860 dollar would be worth multiple times that amount today, but it did not immediately dawn on me that the sums I was seeing regularly in their correspondence—"I draw on you today for fifteen hundred dollars" or "I checked on Farmers Bank of Va yesterday for $2,500" or a reference in 1847 to a $5,000 draft on a Baltimore bank that a Maryland slave trader sent to a Richmond dealer "to have laid out in good No. 1 men"—were so staggering. When I consulted a website maintained by economists at the University of Illinois-Chicago that converts past monetary valuations into present-day purchasing power, I quickly found out just how staggering those sums were. That 1847 Baltimore bank draft of $5,000 forwarded to a Richmond slave trader should be multiplied by 29.70 to get present-day purchasing power: $148,500! The top price for a slave listed on the August 1860 Betts & Gregory price list, $1,625 for "Extra Men," should be multiplied by 29.40 to translate that sum into 2016 purchasing power: $47,775 (an annual middle-class salary in many parts of the United States today).[16]

The total monetary value of the South's entire slave property on the eve of the Civil War was equally stunning. Four billion dollars was the figure given by Commissioner Stephen F. Hale of Alabama to the governor of Kentucky in 1860, and I had come to the conclusion that Hale's valuation was an accurate one. Applying the 2016 multiplier of 29.40 to that four billion 1860 dollars produces a valuation of well over 100 billion dollars today.

These figures took on added significance for me when I was able to calculate the annual sales of a Richmond slave dealer in the late 1850s. These were boom years in the Richmond trade, and Hector Davis (a dealer whose sales books for the years 1857–65 are in the manuscript holdings of the Chicago History Museum) was a major, but by no means the largest, Richmond trader. The sales of Hector Davis & Co. in 1858 totaled $1,773,251; in 1859, they totaled $2,671,572. It thus was by no means a stretch for me to conclude that total slave sales in Richmond in 1859 could easily have reached seven or eight million dollars, and that those figures were probably a low estimate. So, to repeat, Commissioner Henry Benning would seem to have known exactly what he was doing when he made the decision to close his convention address with a lengthy discussion of the slave trade.[17]

One of the most astute delegates sitting on the floor of the Virginia convention the day Benning spoke was a lawyer from the

Rockbridge County town of Lexington named Samuel McDowell Moore. Moore had a long and distinguished political career in the commonwealth: member of the Virginia House of Delegates from 1825 to 1833; a supporter of democratic reforms in the Virginia Constitutional Convention of 1829–30; Whig congressman in the United States House of Representatives from 1833 to 1835; and member of the Virginia House of Delegates again and then the state senate in the late 1830s and the 1840s. Moore had reached an age—he had turned sixty-four exactly four days before Benning spoke—where he had witnessed decades of mounting sectional tension that threatened to destroy the Union, and he wanted no part of the secession movement. He had stood as a Unionist candidate in the February 4 election to choose delegates to the convention and had won one of Rockbridge County's two seats in that body.[18]

During the weeks the convention was in session in Richmond, Moore wrote regular letters to James D. Davidson, a close friend and fellow lawyer back in Lexington; Davidson was also a strong Unionist.

Moore's anxiety mounted as February turned into March and no national compromise emerged and the mood in Richmond became increasingly charged. "Great efforts are being made, by the secessionists, to get up excitement and alarm among the people, to induce them to instruct their Delegates in the Convention, to vote for immediate secession," he wrote Davidson on March 10. "We have no newspaper in this City favoring our views, whilst the other side have the Enquirer, Examiner, Dispatch & S[outhern] Lit[erary] Messenger, and The Whig, about half the time." The "sensation lies and letters" published in the Richmond press were clearly intended "to excite alarm, and drive the people to madness," Moore claimed. "This City is controlled by a mob, who parade the streets insulting the [Unionist] Delegates to the Convention."

When Moore learned that a previously strong Unionist voice

back home, the *Lexington Valley Star*, had changed management and gone over to the radical side, he suspected the worst. "I suppose the negro traders furnished the money to buy the Star," he wrote Davidson on March 29. "I think they are buying up most of the presses in the state," and it was rumored in Richmond that "the Whig is to come out for secession next week."

By early the next month, Moore's gloom had deepened. "The friends of the Union, have great difficulties to contend with," he told Davidson on April 6. "Every newspaper in the City is against us, and a false coloring is given to all our proceedings, in order to deceive the people." And Moore was sure he knew who to blame. "The most of the difficulties we have to contend with, arise from the powerful influence exerted by the most potent money power, that ever has existed in Virginia," he continued. "I mean the power of the Traders in negroes." The rest of Moore's commentary on "the Traders in negroes" deserves to be quoted in full:

> They own a Bank in this City, and have millions of money under their control. (It is said that the profits of one trader here, in the last year, were over a hundred thousand dollars.) The interest of these people is entirely with the seceded states, and to promote it, they would sacrifice every other interest in the state, without the least scruple. And I have reason to believe, they are spending their money freely, in order to influence the public mind in favor of immediate secession. It is known that the mobs gotten up here to parade the streets, and insult the Union men in the Convention, was gotten up by them. They are buying up presses, and among them, I see the Valley Star has been purchased.

Moore identified by name a prominent Rockbridge County slave trader as the most likely purchaser of the *Valley Star*.[19]

Moore's indictment of Virginia's "Traders in negroes" is fascinating and suggestive. He was, to repeat, an experienced political hand in the commonwealth, and he was present, both on the convention floor and in the city of Richmond more generally, as the crisis of the Union reached its climax. And he was convinced that the slave traders were doing everything in their power to make sure that the threat raised by Henry Benning in his February convention address—to bar the sale of Virginia's slaves in the new Confederate States—would not be realized.

How much weight should we assign to these economic factors as we try to explain the coming of the Civil War?

In *Apostles of Disunion*, when I cited the December 1860 speech given by Alabama commissioners Isham W. Garrott and Robert Hardy Smith to the North Carolina legislature, I followed my reporting of their comments on the foreign and domestic slave trade with this observation: "A shared economic interest in slavery, and the internal slave trade, was a subject of some importance, but it was by no means the central issue."[20]

I still stand by that analysis. My basic argument was, and still is, that the commissioners fanning out across the South in late 1860 and early 1861 insisted that emancipation, led by an abolitionist President Lincoln and his Black Republican administration, would plunge their beloved Southland into a nightmare world: unthinkable racial equality, an apocalyptic race war that would drench their region in blood, and a widespread black sexual assault on white women that would destroy the purity of the white race. It was this horrific vision that lay at the heart of the secession persuasion in the Deep South in 1860–61. I became even more convinced of the validity of that interpretation as I came to grips with my own story of where I grew up, how I was raised, and what I came to believe about race in the Jim Crow South, the story I attempted to tell in *The Making of a Racist.*

But I have also come to believe that economic considerations deserved more discussion than I had originally given them. Material prosperity, and the labor system and the trade in human beings that sustained that prosperity, figured in the story as well—not as the very core of the secessionist mindset, but an important factor in the drive to destroy the Union in those dark days at the end of 1860 and the beginning of 1861.

Indeed, how could they not consider the economic consequences of emancipation? The two largest industries in the Old South were staple crop agriculture and the slave trade. No other economic activity came even close to these two enterprises. So they had to figure in the secession commissioners' argument, and they did.

As I was reading back through the messages the commissioners delivered across the South in 1860–61, I found that I had overlooked one important document, one that discussed the all-important relationship between the institution of slavery, the present booming Southern economy, and the even greater material benefits that would follow in the wake of secession. This document was the letter submitted by Commissioner George Williamson of Louisiana to the Texas State Convention in February 1861.

Williamson was the only commissioner sent out by Louisiana, and his letter to the Texas convention was dated February 11, 1861. The Texas delegates had adopted their secession ordinance ten days earlier, on February 1, so Commissioner Williamson had arrived a bit late to the party, as it were. His comments had taken on less significance to me largely because of that factor, but I should have paid more attention to what he had to say.

George Williamson, like many of the commissioners, was not a major political figure in his adopted state of Louisiana. He was born in South Carolina in 1829 and had relocated with his family to Louisiana, where his father operated a steamboat on the Red River and was one of the founders of the town of Shreveport in 1835. George returned to South Carolina for his college education, graduating from the University of South Carolina in 1850, and then set up a law practice in Shreveport and nearby Mansfield, two towns very close to the Texas border. He acquired a plantation near Shreveport in neighboring DeSoto Parish, bought slaves to work that property, and began building a political career. In 1861, he was serving as Caddo Parish attorney when he was elected to a seat in the Louisiana State Convention as an Immediate Secessionist. The convention chose him to serve as Louisiana's commissioner to Texas, a logical choice given the location of his base of operations: the western boundary of Caddo and DeSoto Parishes is the eastern boundary of the state of Texas.[21]

The Texas convention was not in session when Williamson arrived in Austin, so he transmitted his thoughts in a letter to Oran M. Roberts, the president of the convention. It was clear, Williamson insisted, that Abraham Lincoln, "a stalwart fanatic of the Northwest," supported "by the frenzied bigotry of [the Northern] unpatriotic masses," was preparing an assault on the "liberties and property" of the citizens of his adopted state. Louisiana, as a consequence, had boldly taken the path of secession. She now "looks to the formation of a Southern confederacy to preserve the blessings of African slavery, and of the free institutions of the founders of the [original] Federal Union."

It was at this point in his letter that Williamson turned to the economic ties that bound the two states together. "Louisiana and Texas have the same language, laws, and institutions," he wrote. "They grow the same great staples—sugar and cotton," and their people enjoy "the most cordial social and commercial intercourse." Two great rivers, the Sabine and the Red, "form common highways for the transportation of their produce [read, principally: cotton] to the markets of the world [read, principally: Great Britain]." Williamson made specific reference to the fact that "the banks of New Orleans furnish Texas with her only paper circulating medium," and "both States have large areas of fertile, uncultivated lands, peculiarly adapted to slave labor; and they are both so deeply interested in African slavery that it may be said to be absolutely necessary to their existence, and is the keystone to the arch of their prosperity."

This was not empty rhetoric on Williamson's part. As recent scholarship has made clear, the links between Southern, and indeed Northern, financial institutions and the production and marketing of the South's great staple crops (as well as the interstate slave trade, which Williamson did not mention specifically) were absolutely vital to the economic growth and prosperity of the region, and these factors collectively played a major role in the development of American capitalism itself in the nineteenth century.[22]

"The people of Louisiana would consider it a most fatal blow to African slavery, if Texas either did not secede or having seceded should not join her destinies to theirs in a Southern Confederacy," Williamson continued. Dire calamities—"incendiarism and murder"—would follow such failures. "The people of the slave-holding States are bound together by the same necessity and determination to preserve African slavery," he concluded; "we hope to form a slave-holding confederacy that will secure to us and our remotest posterity the great blessings its authors designed in the [old] Federal Union." And since "the social balance wheel of slavery" was available "to regulate its machinery," the new nation, the Confederate States of America, "will be perpetual."[23]

Williamson's words are worth listening to. His clear emphasis on "African slavery" as "the keystone to the arch of their prosperity" was simply a recognition of the profoundly important role the institution played in the economic life of the Old South. But slavery was much more than that, of course. It guaranteed whites social and physical control over what they believed was an alien, brutish, and inferior people. It kept a potential race war in check. It protected white womanhood. It sustained white supremacy. Slavery was at the core, the very heart, of their society and culture. It dominated their politics, it was sustained by their churches, and, as Williamson went to great lengths to suggest, it fueled their economy.

All of these things mattered. But the things that mattered most all came back to race. That is where the crux of the secession persuasion that gripped the Deep South in 1860–61 lay. Mississippi commissioner William L. Harris said it with remarkable clarity. As he told the Georgia legislature on December 17, 1860, Mississippi "had rather see the last of her race, men, women and children, immolated in one common funeral pile, than see them subjected to the degradation of civil, political and social equality with the negro race."[24]

The message Alabama's Stephen F. Hale conveyed to the governor of Kentucky ten days after Judge Harris addressed the Georgians was just as clear and just as powerful. "What Southern man," he asked, "be he slave-holder or non-slave-holder, can without indignation and horror contemplate the triumph of negro equality, and see his own sons and daughters in the not distant future associating with free negroes upon terms of political and social equality, and the white man stripped by the heaven-daring hand of fanaticism of that title to superiority over the black race which God himself has bestowed."[25]

On the day I composed the paragraph just above, my morning newspaper carried an article headlined "Down in Dixie: Bill would stop removal of Confederate, historic markers." Datelined Montgomery, Alabama, this Associated Press report covered the details of a bill proposed by Republican state senator Gerald Allen of Tuscaloosa "that would prohibit the removal of historic monuments, plaques and statues from public property unless a committee of [Alabama state] lawmakers grants a waiver." In testifying on behalf of his bill at a public hearing, Senator Allen is quoted as saying, "I think there is an undercurrent, not just in Alabama, but throughout the nation" among people whose aim is "to kind of rewrite history or whitewash it." He denied his bill was designed solely to protect Confederate monuments, but his proposal came after civic leaders in Birmingham, a city with an African American majority, had raised "the possibility of removing a Confederate memorial from a downtown park." The article went on to note that Republican governor Robert Bentley had "removed four Confederate flags last year from the grounds of the Alabama Capitol," but that the governor indicated that "he had no plans to remove an 88-foot-tall Confederate monument that stands outside his office."

Senator Allen's bill was greeted enthusiastically by Mike Williams, a member of the Alabama Sons of Confederate Veterans, who said these monuments only honor those who "answered the call of duty for their state." And, he added, do not "disgrace my grandfathers or these people's grandfathers by allowing political correctness to come into this state and start destroying the history of this country."

Not surprisingly, some black Alabamians took exception to Senator Allen's proposal. "Nobody wants to erase history, but there are always two sides to that story," the Reverend Rayford Mack of the Montgomery branch of the National Association for the Advancement of Colored People is quoted as saying. "If this monument is in the middle of a predominately black area, or a predominately minority area, how do you think that makes the community feel?" he asked. "How can I take pride in something that wanted to continue my enslavement?"[26]

And so the argument over secession, the causes of the Civil War, and the honor, or dishonor, that should be accorded the Confederate States of America continues. Back in 2001 in chapter 1 of this book, I wrote that, in contrast to "present-day South Africa, the nineteenth-century South saw no Truth and Reconciliation Commission established at the end of the Civil War to investigate the causes of that bloody conflict."[27] In a remarkable editorial published in 2015 in the wake of the Emanuel A.M.E. Church killings, the reliably conservative *Richmond Times-Dispatch* issued a call for just such a commission. No real accounting of the South's racial history had ever taken place, the editorial pointed out; "the half remains untold." Our country "has not authorized a truth and reconciliation commission." The election of Barack Obama as president of the United States "did not translate into a post-racial society." Americans on the white side of the color line seem to believe "that the Civil Rights Act of 1964 and the Voting Rights Act of 1965 erased history. Several centuries of slavery followed by segregation and racism, de jure and de facto, apparently left no trace," the editorial continued. "Nothing could be less conservative than a reluctance to confront the past."

The editorial called on the commonwealth to lead the way in this healing process. "Virginia is the ideal state to take the lead in addressing truth and reconciliation." The state and the city of Richmond have both the "resources and passion" necessary for such an effort. "Taking command of a truth and reconciliation process" would transform the Old Dominion into something new, "the Dynamic Dominion," and it would do so "in sublime ways."[28]

As of this writing, Virginians have not answered this call. Nor have other southerners. But such a truth and reconciliation commission is not beyond our reach. And such a group could well start by answering, honestly and forthrightly, the question posed in the first line and the last line of chapter 1 of this book: "The Civil War was fought over what important issue?"

Appendix

DOCUMENT I

Address of William L. Harris, commissioner from Mississippi, to the Georgia General Assembly, Dec. 17, 1860. This speech was published in pamphlet form as *Address of Hon. W. L. Harris, Commissioner from the State of Mississippi, Delivered before the General Assembly of the State of Georgia, on Monday, Dec. 17th, 1860* (Milledgeville, Ga., 1860), copy at the State Historical Society of Wisconsin.

Mr. President, and gentlemen of the Senate and House of Representatives of the State of Georgia:

I am profoundly sensible of the delicate and important duty imposed upon me, by the courtesy of this public reception.

Under different circumstances, it would have afforded me great pleasure, as a native Georgian—reared and educated on her soil—to express to you fully, the views which prevail in my native State, in relation to the great measures of deliverance and relief from the principles and policy of the new Administration, which are there in progress.

I cannot consent, however, upon the very heel of your arduous and exciting session, to avail myself of your respectful courtesy to the State I have the honor to represent, as well as your personal kindness to her humble representative, to prolong the discussion of a subject which, however, important and absorbing, has, doubtless, been already exhausted in your hearing, by some of the first intellects of your State, if not of the nation.

I beg, therefore, to refer you to the action of Mississippi—already submitted to your Executive—to ask for her the sympathy and co-operation she seeks for the common good, and briefly to suggest to you some of the motives which influence her conduct.

I am instructed by the resolution from which I derive my mission, to inform the State of Georgia, that Mississippi has passed an act calling a convention of her people, "to consider the present threatening relations of the Northern and Southern sections of the Confederacy—*aggravated* by the recent election of a President, upon principles of hostility to the States of the South; and to express the *earnest* hope of Mississippi, that this State will co-operate with her in the adoption of *efficient measures* for their common defence and safety."

It will be remembered, that the violation of our constitutional rights, which has caused such universal dissatisfaction in the South, is not of recent date. Ten years since, this Union was rocked from centre to circumference, by the very same outrages, of which we now complain, only now "aggravated" by the recent election. Nothing but her devotion to the Union our Fathers made, induced the South, *then,* to yield to a compromise, in which Mr. Clay rightly said, we had yielded everything but our honor. We had then in Mississippi a warm contest, which finally ended in reluctant acquiescence in the Compromise measures. The North pledged anew her faith to yield to us our constitutional rights in relation to slave property. They are now, and have been ever since that act, denied to us, until her broken faith and impudent threats, had become almost insufferable *before* the late election.

There were three candidates presented to the North by Southern men, all of whom represented the last degree of conservatism and concession, which their respective parties were willing to yield, to appease the fanaticism of the North. Some of them were scarcely deemed sound, in the South, on the slavery question, and none of them suited our ultra men. And yet the North rejected them all; and their *united* voice, both before and since their overwhelming triumph in this election, has been more defiant and more intolerant than ever before. They have demanded, and now demand, equality between the white and negro races, under our Constitution; equality in representation, equality in the right of suffrage, equality in the honors and emoluments of office, equality in the social circle, equality in the rights of matrimony. The cry has been, and now is, "that slavery must cease, or American liberty must perish," that "the success of Black Republicanism is the triumph of anti-slavery," "a revolution in the tendencies of the government that must be carried out."

To-day our government stands *totally revolutionized* in its main features, and our Constitution broken and overturned. The new administration, which has effected this revolution, only awaits the 4th of March for the inauguration of the new government, the new principles, and the new policy, upon the success of which they have proclaimed freedom to the slave, but eternal degradation for you and for us.

No revolution was ever more complete, though bloodless, if you will tamely submit to the destruction of that Constitution and that Union our fathers made.

Our fathers made this a government for the white man, rejecting the negro, as an ignorant, inferior, barbarian race, incapable of self-government, and not, therefore, entitled to be associated with the white man upon terms of civil, political, or social equality.

This new administration comes into power, under the solemn pledge to overturn and strike down this great feature of our Union, without which it would never have been formed, and to substitute in its stead their new theory of the universal equality of the black and white races.

Our fathers secured to us, by our Constitutional Union, now being overturned by this Black Republican rule, protection to life, liberty and property, *all over the Union,* and wherever its flag was unfurled, whether on land or sea.

Under this wretched, lawless spirit and policy, now usurping the control of that government, citizens of the South have been deprived of their property, and for attempting to seek the redress promised by the compromise laws, have lost their liberty and their lives.

Equality of rights secured to white men, in equal sovereign States, is among the most prominent features of the Constitution under which we have so long lived.

This equality has been denied us in the South for years in the common territories, while the North has virtually distributed them as bounties to abolition fanatics and foreigners, for their brigand service in aiding in our exclusion.

Our Constitution, in unmistakable language, guarantees the return of our fugitive slaves. Congress has recognized her duty in this respect, by enacting proper laws for the enforcement of this right.

And yet these laws have been continually nullified, and the solemn pledge of the Compromise of 1850, by which the North came under renewed obligations to enforce them, has been faithlessly disregarded, and the government and its officers set at defiance.

Who now expects these rebels against the laws passed by their own consent and procurement—rebels against justice and common honesty—to become pious patriots by the acquisition of power? Who now expects Mr. Lincoln to become conservative, when the only secret of his success, and the only foundation of his authority, is the will and command of that robber clan, whose mere instrument he is, who have achieved this revolution in our government by treading under their unhallowed feet our Constitution and laws and the Union of our fathers, and by openly defying high heaven by wilful and corrupt perjury?

And, above all, who is it in the South, born or descended of Revolutionary sires, *who so loves such company,* as that he will long hesitate before he can obtain the consent of a virtuous and patriotic heart and conscience to separate from them *forever?*

Mississippi is firmly convinced that there is but one alternative:

This *new union* with Lincoln Black Republicans and free negroes, *without slavery;* or, slavery under our old constitutional bond of union, *without* Lincoln Black Republicans, or free negroes either, to molest us.

If we take the former, then submission to negro equality is our fate. If the latter, then *secession* is inevitable—each State for itself and by itself, but with a view to the immediate formation of a Southern Confederacy, under our present Constitution, by such of the slave-holding States as shall agree in their conventions to unite with us.

Mississippi seeks no delay—the issue is not new to her people. They have long and anxiously watched its approach—they think it too late, now, to negotiate more compromises with bankrupts in political integrity whose recreancy to justice, good faith and constitutional obligations is the most cherished feature of their political organization.

She has exhausted her rights in sacrificial offerings to save the Union, until nearly all is lost but her honor and the courage to defend it. She has tried conventions until they have become the ridicule of both our friends and our enemies—mere instruments of fraudulent evasion and delay, to wear out the spirit of our people and encourage the hopes of our common enemy. In short, she is sick and tired of the North, and pants for some respite from eternal disturbance and disquiet.

She comes now to you,—our glorious old mother,—the land of Baldwin, who first defiantly asserted and preserved your rights as to slavery, in the federal convention, in opposition to Messrs. Madison, Mason, and Randolph, and the whole Union except the two Carolinas,—the land of Jackson, who immortalized himself by his bold exposure and successful overthrow of a legislative fraud and usurpation upon the rights of the people,—the land of Troup, the sternest Roman of them all, who, single-handed and alone, without co-operation, without consultation, but with truth and justice, and the courage of freemen at home on his side, defied this National Government in its usurpations on the rights of Georgia, and executed your laws in spite of the threats of Federal coercion. It is to you we come,—the brightest exemplar among the advocates and defenders of State rights and State remedies,—to take counsel and solicit sympathy in this hour of our common trial.

I ask you, shall Mississippi follow in the footsteps of Georgia, when led by her gallant Troup? Or, is it reserved for this generation to repudiate and expunge the brightest page in the history of my native State? Impossible! God forbid it! Forbid it, ye people of all Northern and Western Georgia, who, to-day, owe your existence and unparalleled prosperity to the maintenance of your rights at the risk of civil war.

I see around me some gallant spirits who bore their share in the dangers, and now wear with honor, here to-day in this Hall the laurels won on the side of their State, under the banner, inscribed "Troup and the treaty" in that memorable struggle. Need I appeal to them in behalf of my adopted State, to know on what side they will range themselves in this struggle of right, against assumption of brute force, against the Constitutional rights of a sister of this confederacy of equal States? I make no such appeal; I *know* where you stand. To doubt it would be to offer you the grossest insult.

In this school of old republican orthodoxy, I drew my first breath. It was here, I first studied, then embraced, and next feebly advocated the principle of State Rights and State remedies of resistance to tyranny—of the supremacy and sovereignty of the people of a State, and the subserviency of governments to their peace and happiness and safety. These principles will descend with me to the grave, when this frail tenement of dust must perish; but *they* will live on with time, and only perish when tyranny shall be no more.

I need not remind your great State, that thousands and thousands of her sons and daughters, who have sought and found happy homes and prosperous fortunes in the distant forests of her old colonial domain, though now adopted children of Mississippi, still cling with the fond embrace of filial love to this old mother of States and of statesmen, from whom both they and their adopted State derive their origin. It will be difficult for such to *conceive*, that they are not still the objects of your kind solicitude and maternal sympathy.

Mississippi indulges the *most confident expectation and belief,* founded on sources of information she cannot doubt, as well as on the existence of causes, operating upon them, alike as upon her, that every other Gulf State will stand by her side in defence of the position she is about to assume; and she would reproach herself, and every Georgia son within her limits, would swell with indignation, if she hesitated to believe that Georgia too, would blend *her* fate with her natural friends; her sons and daughters—her neighboring sisters in the impending struggle.

Whatever may be the result of your deliberations, I beg to assure her from my intimate knowledge of the spirit and affections of our people, that no enemy to *her* constitutional rights, may consider his victory won, while a Mississippian lives to prolong the contest. Sink or swim, live or die, survive or perish, the part of Mississippi is chosen, *she will never submit* to the principles and policy of this Black Republican Administration.

She had rather see the last of her race, men, women and children, immolated in one common funeral pile, than see them subjected to the degradation of civil, political and social equality with the negro race.

DOCUMENT 2

Letter of Stephen F. Hale, commissioner from Alabama, to Governor
Beriah Magoffin of Kentucky, Dec. 27, 1860. This document can be
found in *OR,* ser. 4, 1:4–11.

FRANKFORT, *December 27, 1860.*

His Excellency B. MAGOFFIN,

    Governor of the Commonwealth of Kentucky:

I have the honor of placing in your hands herewith a commission
from the Governor of the State of Alabama, accrediting me as a
commissioner from that State to the sovereign State of Kentucky, to
consult in reference to the momentous issues now pending between
the Northern and Southern States of this confederacy. Although each
State, as a sovereign political community, must finally determine
these grave issues for itself, yet the identity of interests, sympathy, and
institutions, prevailing alike in all of the slave-holding States, in the
opinion of Alabama renders it proper that there should be a frank and
friendly consultation by each one with her sister Southern States
touching their common grievances and the measures necessary to be
adopted to protect the interest, honor, and safety of their citizens. I
come, then, in a spirit of fraternity, as the commissioner on the part
of the State of Alabama, to confer with the authorities of this Commonwealth in reference to the infraction of our constitutional rights,
wrongs done and threatened to be done, as well as the mode and
measure of redress proper to be adopted by the sovereign States aggrieved to preserve their sovereignty, vindicate their rights, and protect their citizens. In order to a clear understanding of the appropriate
remedy, it may be proper to consider the rights and duties, both of
the State and citizen, under the Federal compact, as well as the
wrongs done and threatened. I therefore submit for the consideration

of Your Excellency the following propositions, which I hope will command your assent and approval:

1. The people are the source of all political power, and the primary object of all good governments is to protect the citizen in the enjoyment of life, liberty, and property; and whenever any form of government becomes destructive of these ends, it is the inalienable right and the duty of the people to alter or abolish it.

2. The equality of all the States of this confederacy, as well as the equality of rights of all the citizens of the respective States under the Federal Constitution, is a fundamental principle in the scheme of the federal government. The union of these States under the Constitution as formed "to establish justice, insure domestic tranquility, provide for the common defense, promote the general welfare, and secure the blessings of liberty to her citizens and their posterity;" and when it is perverted to the destruction of the equality of the States, or substantially fails to accomplish these ends, it fails to achieve the purposes of its creation, and ought to be dissolved.

3. The Federal Government results from a compact entered into between separate, sovereign, and independent States, called the Constitution of the United States, and amendments thereto, by which these sovereign States delegated certain specific powers to be used by that Government for the common defense and general welfare of all the States and their citizens; and when these powers are abused, or used for the destruction of the rights of any State or its citizens, each State has an equal right to judge for itself as well of the violations and infractions of that instrument as of the mode and measure of redress; and if the interest or safety of her citizens demands it, may resume the powers she had delegated without let or hindrance from the Federal Government or any other power on earth.

4. Each State is bound in good faith to observe and keep on her

part all the stipulations and covenants inserted for the benefit of other States in the constitutional compact (the only bond of union by which the several States are bound together), and when persistently violated by one party to the prejudice of her sister States, ceases to be obligatory on the States so aggrieved, and they may rightfully declare the compact broken, the union thereby formed dissolved, and stand upon their original rights as sovereign and independent political communities; and further, that each citizen owes his primary allegiance to the State in which he resides, and hence it is the imperative duty of the State to protect him in the enjoyment of all his constitutional rights, and see to it that they are not denied or withheld from him with impunity by any other State or government.

If the foregoing propositions correctly indicate the objects of this government, the rights and duties of the citizen, as well as the rights, powers, and duties of the State and Federal Governments under the Constitution, the next inquiry is, what rights have been denied, what wrongs have been done, or threatened to be done, of which the Southern States or the people of the Southern States can complain?

At the time of the adoption of the Federal Constitution African slavery existed in twelve of the thirteen States. Slaves are recognized both as property and as a basis of political power by the Federal compact, and special provisions are made by that instrument for their protection as property. Under the influences of climate and other causes, slavery has been banished from the Northern States; the slaves themselves have been sent to the Southern States and there sold, and their price gone into the pockets of their former owners at the North. And in the meantime African slavery has not only become one of the fixed domestic institutions of the Southern States, but forms an important element of their political power, and constitutes the most valuable species of their property, worth, according to recent estimates, not less than $4,000,000,000; forming, in fact, the basis upon which rests the prosperity and wealth of most of these States, and supplying the commerce of the world with its richest freights, and furnishing the manufactories of two continents with the raw material, and their operatives with bread. It is upon this gigantic interest, this peculiar institution of the South, that the Northern States and their people have been waging an unrelenting and fanatical war for the last quarter of a century; an institution with which is bound up not only the wealth and prosperity of the Southern people, but their very existence as a political community. This war has been waged in every way that human ingenuity, urged on by fanaticism, could suggest. They attack us through their literature, in their schools, from the hustings, in their legislative halls, through the public press, and even their courts of justice forget the purity of their judicial ermine to strike down the rights of the Southern slave-holder and override every barrier which the Constitution has erected for his protection; and the sacred desk is desecrated to this unholy crusade against our lives, our property, and the constitutional rights guaranteed to us by the compact of our fathers. During all this time the Southern States have freely conceded to the Northern States and the people of those States every right secured to them by the Constitution, and an equal interest in the common territories of the Government; protected the lives and property of their citizens of every kind, when brought within Southern jurisdiction; enforced through their courts, when necessary, every law of Congress passed for the protection of Northern property, and submitted ever since the foundation of the Government, with scarcely a murmur, to the protection of their shipping, manufacturing, and commercial interests, by odious bounties, discriminating tariffs, and unjust navigation laws, passed by the Federal Government to the prejudice and injury of their own citizens.

The law of Congress for the rendition of fugitive slaves, passed in pursuance of an express provision of the Constitution, remains almost a dead letter upon the statute book. A majority of the Northern States, through their legislative enactments, have openly nullified it, and impose heavy fines and penalties upon all persons who aid in enforcing this law, and some of those States declare the Southern slave-holder who goes within their jurisdiction to assert his legal rights under the Constitution guilty of a high crime, and affix imprisonment in the penitentiary as the penalty. The Federal officers who attempt to discharge their duties under the law, as well as the owner of the slave, are set upon by mobs, and are fortunate if they escape without serious injury to life or limb; and the State authorities, instead of aiding in the enforcement of this law, refuse the use of their jails, and by every means which unprincipled fanaticism can devise give countenance to the mob and aid the fugitive to escape. Thus there are annually large amounts of property actually stolen away from the Southern States, harbored and protected in Northern States and by their citizens; and when a requisition is made for the thief by the Governor of a Southern State upon the Executive of a Northern State, in pursuance of the express conditions of the Federal Constitution, he is insultingly told that the felon has committed no crime, and thus the criminal escapes, the property of the citizen is lost, the sovereignty of the State is insulted, and there is no redress, for the Federal courts have no jurisdiction to award a mandamus to the Governor of a sovereign State to compel him to do an official executive act, and Congress, if disposed, under the Constitution has no power to afford a remedy. These are wrongs under which the Southern people have long suffered, and to which they have patiently submitted, in the hope that a returning sense of justice would prompt the people of the Northern States to discharge their constitutional obligations and save our common country. Recent events, however, have not justified their hopes. The more daring and restless fanatics have banded themselves together, have put in practice the terrible lessons taught by the timid by making an armed incursion upon the sovereign State of Virginia, slaughtering her citizens, for the purpose of exciting a servile insurrection among her slave population, and arming them for the destruction of their own masters. During the past summer the abolition incendiary has lit up the prairies of Texas, fired the dwellings of the inhabitants, burned down whole towns, and laid poison for her citizens, thus literally executing the terrible denunciations of fanaticism against the slave-holder, "Alarm to their sleep, fire to their dwellings, and poison to their food."

The same fell spirit, like an unchained demon, has for years swept over the plains of Kansas, leaving death, desolation, and ruin in its track. Nor is this the mere ebullition of a few half-crazy fanatics, as is abundantly apparent from the sympathy manifested all over the North, where, in many places, the tragic death of John Brown, the leader of the raid upon Virginia, who died upon the gallows a condemned felon, is celebrated with public honors, and his name canonized as a martyr to liberty; and many, even of the more conservative papers of the Black Republican school, were accustomed to speak of his murderous attack upon the lives of the unsuspecting citizens of Virginia in a half-sneering and half-apologetic tone. And what has the Federal Government done in the meantime to protect slave property upon the common territories of the Union? Whilst a whole squadron of the American Navy is maintained on the coast of Africa at an enormous expense to enforce the execution of the laws against the slave-trade (and properly, too), and the whole Navy is kept afloat to protect the lives and property of American citizens upon the high seas, not a law has been passed by Congress or an arm raised by the Federal Government to protect the slave property of citizens from Southern States upon the soil of Kansas, the common territory and common property of the citizens of all the States, purchased alike by their common treasure, and held by the Federal Government, as declared by the Supreme Court of the United States, as the trustee for all their citizens; but, upon the contrary, a territorial government, created by Congress and supported out of the common treasury, under the influence and control of emigrant-aid societies and abolition emissaries, is permitted to pass laws excluding and destroying all that species of property within her limits, thus ignoring on the part of the Federal Government one of the fundamental principles of all good governments—the duty to protect the property of the citizen—and wholly refusing to maintain the equal rights of the States and the citizens of the States upon their common territories.

As the last and crowning act of insult and outrage upon the people of the South, the citizens of the Northern States, by overwhelming majorities, on the 6th day of November last, elected Abraham Lincoln and Hannibal Hamlin President and Vice-President of the United States. Whilst it may be admitted that the mere election of any man to the Presidency is not *per se* a sufficient cause for a dissolution of the Union, yet when the issues upon and circumstances under which he was elected are properly appreciated and understood, the question arises whether a due regard to the interest, honor, and safety of their citizens, in view of this and all the other antecedent wrongs and outrages, do not render it the imperative duty of the Southern States to resume the powers they have delegated to the Federal Government and interpose their sovereignty for the protection of their citizens.

What, then, are the circumstances under which and the issues upon which he was elected? His own declarations and the current history of the times but too plainly indicate he was elected by a Northern sectional vote, against the most solemn warnings and protestations of the whole South. He stands forth as the representative of the fanaticism of the North, which, for the last quarter of a century, has been making war upon the South, her property, her civilization, her institutions, and her interests; as the representative of that party which overrides all constitutional barriers, ignores the obligation of official oaths, and acknowledges allegiance to a higher law than the Constitution, striking down the sovereignty and equality of the States, and resting its claims to popular favor upon the one dogma—the equality of the races, white and black.

It was upon this acknowledgment of allegiance to a higher law that Mr. Seward rested his claims to the Presidency in a speech made by him in Boston before the election. He is the exponent, if not the author, of the doctrine of the irrepressible conflict between freedom and slavery, and proposes that the opponents of slavery shall arrest its further expansion, and by Congressional legislation exclude it from the common territories of the Federal Government, and place it where the public mind shall rest in the belief that it is in the course of ultimate extinction. He claims for free negroes the right of suffrage and an equal voice in the Government; in a word, all the rights of citizenship, although the Federal Constitution, as construed by the highest judicial tribunal in the world, does not recognize Africans imported into this country as slaves or their descendants—whether free or slaves—as citizens.

These were the issues presented in the last Presidential canvass, and upon these the American people passed at the ballot box. Upon the principles then announced by Mr. Lincoln and his leading friends we are bound to expect his administration to be conducted. Hence it is that in high places among the Republican party the election of Mr. Lincoln is hailed not simply as a change of administration, but as the inauguration of new principles and a new theory of government, and even as the downfall of slavery. Therefore it is that the election of Mr. Lincoln cannot be regarded otherwise than a solemn declaration, on the part of a great majority of the Northern people, of hostility to the South, her property, and her institutions; nothing less than an open declaration of war, for the triumph of this new theory of government destroys the property of the South, lays waste her fields, and inaugurates all the horrors of a San Domingo servile insurrection, consigning her citizens to assassinations and her wives and daughters to pollution and violation to gratify the lust of half-civilized Africans. Especially is this true in the cotton-growing States, where, in many localities, the slave outnumbers the white population ten to one.

If the policy of the Republicans is carried out according to the programme indicated by the leaders of the party, and the South submits, degradation and ruin must overwhelm alike all classes of citizens in the Southern States. The slave-holder and non-slave-holder must ultimately share the same fate; all be degraded to a position of equality with free negroes, stand side by side with them at the polls, and fraternize in all the social relations of life, or else there will be an eternal war of races, desolating the land with blood, and utterly wasting and destroying all the resources of the country. Who can look upon such a picture without a shudder? What Southern man, be he slave-holder or non-slave-holder, can without indignation and horror contemplate the triumph of negro equality, and see his own sons and daughters in the not distant future associating with free negroes upon terms of political and social equality, and the white man stripped by the heaven-daring hand of fanaticism of that title to superiority over the black race which God himself has bestowed? In the Northern States, where free negroes are so few as to form no appreciable part of the community, in spite of all the legislation for their protection, they still remain a degraded caste, excluded by the ban of society from social association with all but the lowest and most degraded of the white race. But in the South, where in many places the African race largely predominates, and as a consequence the two races would be continually pressing together, amalgamation or the extermination of the one or the other would be inevitable. Can Southern men submit to such degradation and ruin? God forbid that they should.

But it is said there are many constitutional conservative men at the North who sympathize with and battle for us. That is true; but they are utterly powerless, as the late Presidential election unequivocally shows, to breast the tide of fanaticism that threatens to roll over and crush us. With them it is a question of principle, and we award to them all honor for their loyalty to the Constitution of our fathers; but their defeat is not their ruin. With us it is a question of self-preservation. Our lives, our property, the safety of our homes and our hearthstones, all that men hold dear on earth, is involved in the issue. If we triumph, vindicate our rights, and maintain our institutions, a bright and joyous future lies before us. We can clothe the world with our staple, give wings to her commerce, and supply with bread the starving operative in other lands, and at the same time preserve an institution that has done more to civilize and Christianize the heathen than all human agencies besides—an institution alike beneficial to both races, ameliorating the moral, physical, and intellectual condition of the one and giving wealth and happiness to the other. If we fail, the light of our civilization goes down in blood, our wives and our little ones will be driven from their homes by the light of our own dwellings, the dark pall of barbarism must soon gather over our sunny land, and the scenes of West India emancipation, with its attendant horrors and crimes (that monument of British fanaticism and folly), be re-enacted in their own land upon a more gigantic scale.

Then, is it not time we should be up and doing, like men who know their rights and dare maintain them? To whom shall the people of the Southern States look for the protection of their rights, interests, and honor? We answer, to their own sons and their respective States. To the States, as we have seen, under our system of government, is due the primary allegiance of the citizen, and the correlative obligation of protection devolves upon the respective States—a duty from which they cannot escape, and which they dare not neglect without a violation of all the bonds of fealty that hold together the citizen and the sovereign. The Northern States and their citizens have proved recreant to their obligations under the Federal Constitution. They have violated that compact and refused to perform their covenants in that behalf.

The Federal Government has failed to protect the rights and property of the citizens of the South, and is about to pass into the hands of a party pledged for the destruction not only of their rights and their property, but the equality of the States ordained by the Constitution, and the heaven-ordained superiority of the white over the black race. What remains, then, for the Southern States and the people of these States if they are loyal to the great principles of civil and religious liberty, sanctified by the sufferings of a seven-years' war and baptized with the blood of the Revolution? Can they permit the rights of their citizens to be denied and spurned, their property spirited away, their own sovereignty violated, and themselves degraded to the position of mere dependencies instead of sovereign States; or shall each for itself, judging of the infractions of the constitutional compact, as well as the mode and measure of redress, declare that the covenants of that sacred instrument in their behalf, and for the benefit of their citizens, have been willfully, deliberately, continuously, and persistently broken and violated by the other parties to the compact, and that they and their citizens are therefore absolved from all further obligations to keep and perform the covenants thereof; resume the powers delegated to the Federal Government, and, as sovereign States, form other relations for the protection of their citizens and the discharge of the great ends of government? The union of these States was one of fraternity as well as equality; but what fraternity now exists between the citizens of the two sections? Various religious associations, powerful in number and influence, have been broken asunder, and the sympathies that bound together the people of the several States at the time of the formation of the Constitution have ceased to exist, and feelings of bitterness and even hostility have sprung up in their place. How can this be reconciled and a spirit of fraternity established? Will the people of the North cease to make war upon the institution of slavery and award to it the protection guaranteed by the Constitution? The accumulated wrongs of many years, the late action of their members in Congress refusing every measure of justice to the South, as well as the experience of all the past, answers, No, never!

Will the South give up the institution of slavery and consent that her citizens be stripped of their property, her civilization destroyed, the whole land laid waste by fire and sword? It is impossible. She cannot; she will not. Then why attempt longer to hold together hostile States under the stipulations of a violated Constitution? It is impossible. Disunion is inevitable. Why, then, wait longer for the consummation of a result that must come? Why waste further time in expostulations and appeals to Northern States and their citizens, only to be met, as we have been for years past, by renewed insults and repeated injuries? Will the South be better prepared to meet the emergency when the North shall be strengthened by the admission of the new Territories of Kansas, Nebraska, Washington, Jefferson, Nevada, Idaho, Chippewa, and Arizona as non-slave-holding States, as we are warned from high sources will be done within the next four years, under the administration of Mr. Lincoln? Can the true men at the North ever make a more powerful or successful rally for the preservation of our rights and the Constitution than they did in the last Presidential contest? There is nothing to inspire a hope that they can.

Shall we wait until our enemies shall possess themselves of all the powers of the Government; until abolition judges are on the Supreme Court bench, abolition collectors at every port, and abolition postmasters in every town; secret mail agents traversing the whole land, and a subsidized press established in our midst to demoralize our people? Will we be stronger then or better prepared to meet the struggle, if a struggle must come? No, verily. When that time shall come, well may our adversaries laugh at our folly and deride our impotence. The deliberate judgment of Alabama, as indicated by the joint resolutions of her General Assembly, approved February 24, 1860, is that prudence, patriotism, and loyalty to all the great principles of civil liberty, incorporated in our Constitution and consecrated by the memories of the past, demand that all the Southern States should now resume their delegated powers, maintain the rights, interests, and honor of their citizens, and vindicate their own sovereignty. And she most earnestly but respectfully invites her sister sovereign State, Kentucky, who so gallantly vindicated the sovereignty of the States in 1798, to the consideration of these grave and vital questions, hoping she may concur with the State of Alabama in the conclusions to which she has been driven by the impending dangers that now surround the Southern States. But if, on mature deliberation, she dissents on any point from the conclusions to which the State of Alabama has arrived, on behalf of that State I most respectfully ask a declaration by this venerable Commonwealth of her conclusions and position on all the issues discussed in this communication; and Alabama most respectfully urges upon the people and authorities of Kentucky the startling truth that submission or acquiescence on the part of the Southern States at this perilous hour will enable Black Republicanism to redeem all its nefarious pledges and accomplish all its flagitious ends; and that hesitation or delay in their action will be misconceived and misconstrued by their adversaries and ascribed not to that elevated patriotism that would sacrifice all but their honor to save the Union of their fathers, but to division and dissension among themselves and their consequent weakness; that prompt, bold, and decided action is demanded alike by prudence, patriotism, and the safety of their citizens.

Permit me, in conclusion, on behalf of the State of Alabama, to express my high gratification at the cordial manner in which I have been received as her commissioner by the authorities of the State of Kentucky, as well as the profound personal gratification which, as a son of Kentucky, born and reared within her borders, I feel at the manner in which I, as the commissioner from the State of my adoption, have been received and treated by the authorities of the State of my birth. Please accept assurances of the high consideration and esteem of,

Your obedient servant, &c.,

S. F. HALE,
Commissioner from the State of Alabama.

Notes

Davis
Papers Haskell M. Monroe Jr. et al., eds., *The Papers of Jefferson Davis,* 10 vols. to date (Baton Rouge, La., 1971-).

DAB Allen Johnson et al., eds., *Dictionary of American Biography,* 20 vols. plus Supplements (New York, 1928–96).

OR *The War of the Rebellion: A Compilation of the Official Records of the Union and Confederate Armies,* 128 vols. (Washington, D.C., 1880–1902).

Introduction

1. Michael F. Holt, *The Political Crisis of the 1850s* (New York, 1978); J. Mills Thornton III, *Politics and Power in a Slave Society: Alabama, 1800–1860* (Baton Rouge, La., 1978); Daniel W. Crofts, *Reluctant Confederates: Upper South Unionists in the Secession Crisis* (Chapel Hill, N.C., 1989); Peyton McCrary, Clark Miller, and Dale Baum, "Class and Party in the Secession Crisis: Voting Behavior in the Deep South, 1856–1861," *Journal of Interdisciplinary History* 8 (1978): 429–57.

2. Bertram Wyatt-Brown, *Southern Honor: Ethics and Behavior in the Old South* (New York, 1982) and "Honor and Secession," in *Yankee Saints and Southern Sinners* (Baton Rouge, La., 1985), 183–213; Kenneth S. Greenberg, *Masters and Statesmen: The Political Culture of American Slavery* (Baltimore, 1985).

1. SLAVERY, STATES' RIGHTS, AND SECESSION COMMISSIONERS

1. *Naturalization/Citizenship Notice,* ER-738, BOS, U.S. Department of Justice, Immigration and Naturalization Service, Boston, Mass.

2. *Richmond Times-Dispatch,* July 27, 1999.

3. *Washington Post,* April 10, 1998.

4. Ibid.

5. *New York Times,* Jan. 18, 2000; *Berkshire Eagle* (Pittsfield, Mass.), Jan. 9, 2000.

6. *New York Times,* Jan. 18, 2000.

7. Ibid.

8. Jim Davenport, "6,000 Rally for Confederate Flag" (AP-NY-01-08-00), *AOL News,* Jan. 8, 2000.

9. *Washington Post,* Jan. 9, 2000.

10. Bob Herbert, "Of Flags and Slurs," *New York Times,* Jan. 20, 2000.

11. *Transcript* (North Adams, Mass.), Dec. 28, 1996.

12. *Washington Post National Weekly Edition,* Oct. 13, 1997.

13. *New York Times,* Jan. 18, 2000.

14. Zell Miller, comments to the sixty-fifth annual meeting of the Southern Historical Association, Fort Worth, Texas, Nov. 3, 1999.

15. *Mississippi* 14:1 (Sept.–Oct. 1995): 37.

16. *Atlanta Journal-Constitution,* Aug. 16, 1998. See also Christopher Shea, "Defending Dixie," *Chronicle of Higher Education,* Nov. 10, 1995.

17. Peter Applebome, *Dixie Rising: How the South Is Shaping American Values, Politics, and Culture* (New York, 1996), especially chap. 5, "Columbia, South Carolina: Southern Partisans, Then and Now"; Tony Horwitz, *Confederates in the Attic: Dispatches from the Unfinished Civil War* (New York, 1998).

18. See Thomas J. Pressly, *American Interpret Their Civil War* (Princeton, N.J., 1954); Ralph A. Wooster, "The Secession of the Lower South: An Examination of Changing Interpretations," *Civil War History* 7 (1961): 117–27; William J. Donnelly, "Conspiracy or Popular Movement: The Historiography of Southern Support for Secession," *North Carolina Historical Review* 42

(1965): 70–84; Joel H. Silbey, "The Surge of Republican Power: Partisan Antipathy, American Social Conflict, and the Coming of the Civil War," in *Essays on American Antebellum Politics, 1840–1860,* ed. Stephen E. Maizlish and John J. Kushma (College Station, Tex., 1982), 199–229; James G. Randall, "The Blundering Generation," *Mississippi Valley Historical Review* 47 (1940): 3–28; Eugene D. Genovese, *The Political Economy of Slavery: Studies in the Economy and Society of the Slave South* (New York, 1965); Eric Foner, *Free Soil, Free Labor, Free Men: The Ideology of the Republican Party before the Civil War* (New York, 1970); David M. Potter, *The Impending Crisis, 1848–1861* (New York, 1976); Holt, *Political Crisis of the 1850s;* Thornton, *Politics and Power in a Slave Society;* John McCardell, *The Idea of a Southern Nation: Southern Nationalists and Southern Nationalism, 1830–1860* (New York, 1979); Kenneth M. Stampp, *The Imperiled Union: Essays on the Background of the Civil War* (New York, 1980); Greenberg, *Masters and Statesmen;* Wyatt-Brown, *Southern Honor;* Grady McWhiney, *Cracker Culture: Celtic Ways in the Old South* (Tuscaloosa, Ala., 1988); Gabor S. Boritt, ed., *Why the Civil War Came* (New York, 1996); Michael A. Morrison, *Slavery and the American West: The Eclipse of Manifest Destiny and the Coming of the Civil War* (Chapel Hill, N.C., 1997).

19. Two recent historians who have been particularly eloquent on the role of slavery and race in the coming of the war are Kenneth M. Stampp and George M. Frederickson; see Stampp, *Imperiled Union* and *America in 1857: A Nation on the Brink* (New York, 1990), and Frederickson, *White Supremacy: A Comparative Study in American and South African History* (New York, 1981), especially 150–62.

20. William R. Smith, ed., *The History and Debates of the Convention of the People of Alabama . . . 1861* (Montgomery, Ala., 1861), 76.

21. Ernest W. Winkler, ed., *Journal of the Secession Convention of Texas, 1861* (Austin, Tex., 1912), 35–36.

22. Ibid., 63.

23. *Journal of the Convention of the People of South Carolina, Held in 1860-'61* (Charleston, S.C., 1861), 330–31.

24. *Journal of the Public and Secret Proceedings of the Convention of the People*

of Georgia . . . 1861 (Milledgeville, Ga., 1861), 112–13; William Y. Thompson, *Robert Toombs of Georgia* (Baton Rouge, La., 1966), 159.

25. *Journal of the [Mississippi] State Convention* (Jackson, Miss., 1861), 87–88.

26. *Davis Papers* 7:46–47, 49.

27. "Speech of A. H. Stephens," doc. 48, in Frank Moore, ed., *The Rebellion Record,* 11 vols. (New York, 1864–68), 1:45–46.

28. Hudson Strode, *Jefferson Davis, Confederate President* (New York, 1959), 24.

29. James D. Richardson, ed., *Messages and Papers of the Confederacy,* 2 vols. (Nashville, 1905), 1:67–68.

30. Myrta L. Avary, ed., *Recollections of Alexander H. Stephens: His Diary Kept When a Prisoner at Fort Warren, Boston Harbour, 1865* (rept. Baton Rouge, La., 1998), 172–74.

31. Alexander H. Stephens, *A Constitutional View of the Late War between the States,* 2 vols. (Philadelphia, 1868–70), 1:10–11, 535.

32. Jefferson Davis, *The Rise and Fall of the Confederate Government,* 2 vols. (rept. New York, 1958), 1:xix, 78–80, 83, 2:763.

33. See, e.g., James R. Kennedy and Walter D. Kennedy, *Was Jefferson Davis Right?* (Gretna, La., 1998), 84–85, 255.

34. Scholarship on the commissioners is remarkably thin, and most of the work that has been done centers on the commissioners' role in the calling of the Montgomery Constitutional Convention. See Ellen-Fairbanks D. Diggs, "The Role of the Interstate Commissioners in the Secession Conventions, 1860–1861" (M.A. thesis, University of North Carolina, Chapel Hill, 1947); Armand J. Gerson, "The Inception of the Montgomery Convention," American Historical Association, *Annual Report, 1910* (Washington, D.C., 1912), 181–87; Durward Long, "Alabama's Secession Commissioners," *Civil War History* 9 (1963): 55–66; Charles R. Lee Jr., *The Confederate Constitutions* (Chapel Hill, N.C., 1963), 9–12, 14–16, 18–19.

35. See, e.g., *Address of Hon. W. L. Harris, Commissioner from the State of Mississippi, Delivered before the General Assembly of the State of Georgia, on Monday, Dec. 17th, 1860* (Milledgeville, Ga., 1860); *Speech of the Hon. A. H.*

Handy, Commissioner to Maryland, from the State of Mississippi, Delivered at Princess Anne, on the First Day of January, A.D. 1861 (Jackson, Miss., 1861); *Addresses Delivered before the Virginia State Convention by Hon. Fulton Anderson, Commissioner from Mississippi, Hon. Henry L. Benning, Commissioner from Georgia, and Hon. John S. Preston, Commissioner from South Carolina, February 1861* (Richmond, 1861).

36. See, e.g., Horace Greeley, *The American Conflict*, 2 vols. (Hartford, 1866), 1:344–45, 350; Orville J. Victor, *The History, Civil, Political, and Military, of the Southern Rebellion* (New York, 1861), 22–24, 71, 105, 116, 130, 165, 194–96; Moore, *Rebellion Record* 1:3, 6, 9, 12–13; Benson J. Lossing, *Pictorial History of the Civil War*, 3 vols. (Philadelphia, 1866–68), 1:59, 62, 101, 112, 163, 166, 196; Edward McPherson, *The Political History of the United States of America, during the Great Rebellion* (Washington, D.C., 1864), 2–6, 8, 10–11.

37. *OR*, ser. 4, 1.

38. Dwight L. Dumond, *The Secession Movement, 1860–1861* (New York, 1931), 254.

39. Jon L. Wakelyn, ed., *Southern Pamphlets on Secession, November 1860–April 1861* (Chapel Hill, N.C., 1996), xviii.

2. THE FIRST WAVE

1. "Governor's Message," Nov. 26, 1860, *Journal of the Senate of the State of Mississippi: Called Session [1860]* (Jackson, Miss., 1860), 6, 11, 12.

2. Ibid., 7, 11.

3. *Laws of the State of Mississippi, Passed at a Called Session of the Mississippi Legislature . . . November, 1860* (Jackson, Miss., 1860), 42.

4. Robert W. Dubay, *John Jones Pettus, Mississippi Fire-Eater: His Life and Times, 1813–1867* (Jackson, Miss., 1975), 71.

5. *OR*, ser. 4, 1:30; "Letter from Gov. Moore," Dec. 19, 1860, *Montgomery Daily Mail*, Dec. 20, 1860; Commission of Arthur F. Hopkins and F. M. Gilmer, Dec. 10, 1860, Misc. Letters and Papers, Virginia Executive Papers, Governor John Letcher, Library of Virginia, Richmond; Long, "Alabama's Secession Commissioners," 56–57.

6. Clarence P. Denman, *The Secession Movement in Alabama* (Montgomery, Ala., 1933), 111–12; Long, "Alabama's Secession Commissioners," 57; Smith, *History and Debates . . . Alabama,* 35–36.

7. *Charleston Mercury,* Dec. 17, 1860.

8. E. B. Long, *The Civil War Day by Day: An Almanac, 1861–1865* (Garden City, N.Y., 1971), 3–5.

9. J. A. Elmore to A. B. Moore, Jan. 5, 1861, *OR,* ser. 4, 1:19–20; *Charleston Daily Courier,* Dec. 18, 1860. For biographical data on Elmore, see Willis Brewer, *Alabama: Her History, Resources, War Record, and Public Men* (Montgomery, Ala., 1872), 457–58; William Garrett, *Reminiscences of Public Men in Alabama* (Atlanta, 1872), 61–62; Albert B. Moore, *History of Alabama and Her People,* 3 vols. (Chicago, 1927), 1:570; Thomas M. Owen, *History of Alabama and Dictionary of Alabama Biography,* 4 vols. (Chicago, 1921), 3:541.

10. Charles E. Hooker to John J. Pettus, Jan. 12, 1861, in *Journal of the [Mississippi] State Convention,* 163–64. For biographical data on Hooker, see *Biographical Directory of the American Congress, 1774–1927* (Washington, D.C., 1928), 1111; *Vicksburg Weekly Sun,* Aug. 6, Nov. 5, 1860; *Vicksburg Daily Whig,* Nov. 24, 1860; Dunbar Rowland, *Mississippi: Comprising Sketches of Counties, Towns, Events, Institutions, and Persons,* 3 vols. (Atlanta, 1907), 1:888–89.

11. *Hinds County Gazette* (Raymond, Miss.), Aug. 24, 1859.

12. *Columbia Guardian,* rept. in *Charleston Mercury,* Dec. 17, 1860.

13. *Charleston Mercury,* Dec. 19, 1860.

14. Ibid.

15. For biographical data on Harris, see *DAB* 8:327; Dunbar Rowland, *Courts, Judges, and Lawyers of Mississippi, 1798–1935* (Jackson, Miss., 1935), 78–80, 90–91; James D. Lynch, *The Bench and Bar of Mississippi* (New York, 1881), 342–44; *Davis Papers* 2:195 n. 8.

16. *Milledgeville Federal Union,* Dec. 25, 1860.

17. The Georgia resolution can be found in *Journal of the [Mississippi] State Convention,* 199–201; *New York Times,* Dec. 20, 1860; *Address of Hon. W. L. Harris.*

18. *Athens Southern Banner,* Dec. 27, 1860.

19. For biographical data on Thompson, see *DAB* 18:459–60; P. L. Rainwater, ed., "Letters to and from Jacob Thompson," *Journal of Southern History* 6 (1940): 95–97; *Biographical Directory . . . American Congress,* 1611; Rowland, *Mississippi . . . Sketches* 2:780–82; *Davis Papers* 2:101–2 n. 98.

20. *Natchez Free Trader,* July 13, 1859.

21. J. Thompson to John J. Pettus, Dec. 26, 1860, in *Journal of the [Mississippi] State Convention,* 184–85; *Raleigh State Journal,* Dec. 22, 1860.

22. A. H. Handy to Thomas H. Hicks, Dec. 18, 1860, copy, in Correspondence and Papers of Governor John J. Pettus, Mississippi Department of Archives and History, Jackson; Hicks to Handy, Dec. 19, 1860, in *Journal of the [Mississippi] State Convention,* 181–83; *Baltimore Sun,* Dec. 19, 24, 1860. See also William C. Wright, *The Secession Movement in the Middle Atlantic States* (Rutherford, N.J., 1973), 32–33.

23. For biographical data on Handy, see *DAB* 8:225; Rowland, *Courts, Judges, and Lawyers of Mississippi,* 94–96; Lynch, *Bench and Bar of Mississippi,* 508–10; Rowland, *Mississippi . . . Sketches* 1:836.

24. *Baltimore Sun,* Dec. 20, 1860; *New York Times,* Dec. 20, 1860; *Washington National Intelligencer,* Dec. 21, 1860.

25. For biographical data on Garrott, see Brewer, *Alabama . . . History,* 494–95; Owen, *History of Alabama* 3:640; Garrett, *Reminiscences of Public Men,* 434; Denman, *Secession Movement in Alabama,* 85 n. 44; for biographical data on Smith, see *DAB* 17:339; Brewer, *Alabama . . . History,* 425–26; Owen, *History of Alabama* 4:1592; Garrett, *Reminiscences of Public Men,* 540–42; Ezra J. Warner and W. Buck Yearns, *Biographical Register of the Confederate Congress* (Baton Rouge, La., 1975), 223–24; Thornton, *Politics and Power in a Slave Society,* 433.

26. Smith, *History and Debates . . . Alabama,* 432–36.

3. THE SOUTH CAROLINIANS

1. Maury Klein, *Days of Defiance: Sumter, Secession, and the Coming of the Civil War* (New York, 1997), 145–46; Long, *The Civil War Day by Day,* 13.

2. *Journal of the Convention of the People of South Carolina, Held in 1860, 1861, and 1862, Together with the Ordinances, Reports, Resolutions, etc.* (Columbia, S.C., 1862), 31–32.

3. Laura A. White, *Robert Barnwell Rhett: Father of Secession* (New York, 1931), 145–46, 191–92.

4. *Journal of the Convention . . . South Carolina . . . 1860, 1861, and 1862,* 92–93.

5. Ibid., 126–27.

6. Ibid., 150–51, 153–54, 156–58, 162.

7. Smith, *History and Debates . . . Alabama,* 33; Gerson, "Inception of the Montgomery Convention," 183–85; Lee, *Confederate Constitutions,* 12, 20.

8. *New York Herald,* Jan. 8, 1861.

9. For biographical data on Calhoun, see Owen, *History of Alabama* 2:285; Vicki Vaughn Johnson, *The Men and the Vision of the Southern Commercial Conventions, 1845–1871* (Columbia, Mo., 1992), 75.

10. *Columbia Daily South Carolinian,* Nov. 14, 1860.

11. William K. Scarborough, ed., *The Diary of Edmund Ruffin* 3 vols. (Baton Rouge, La., 1972–89), 1:494.

12. *Columbia Daily South Carolinian,* Nov. 14, 1860.

13. *Charleston Mercury,* Jan. 14, 1861; the speech is also printed in Smith, *History and Debates . . . Alabama,* 31–33.

14. *Memphis Daily Appeal,* Jan. 11, 1861.

15. *OR,* ser. 4, 1:43–44; Lee, *Confederate Constitutions,* 16.

16. Ronald T. Takaki, *A Pro-Slavery Crusade: The Agitation to Reopen the African Slave Trade* (New York, 1971), 1.

17. For biographical data on Spratt, see John A. May and Joan R. Faunt, *South Carolina Secedes* (Columbia, S.C., 1960), 213; Robert Manson Myers, ed., *The Children of Pride: A True Story of Georgia and the Civil War* (New Haven, 1972), 1684; Takaki, *Pro-Slavery Crusade,* 19–21, 215–25; White, *Robert Barnwell Rhett,* 139, 153, 179; Scarborough, *Ruffin Diary* 1:285.

18. *Charleston Mercury,* Jan. 12, 1861.

19. Scarborough, *Ruffin Diary* 1:526.

20. William W. Davis, *The Civil War and Reconstruction in Florida* (New York, 1913), 59–60; Long, *Civil War Day by Day,* 24, 31; Lee, *Confederate Constitutions,* 14–15.

21. Klein, *Days of Defiance,* 154–57, 195–97, 201–3; Long, *Civil War Day by Day,* 15–16, 23, 24.

22. *Journal of the [Mississippi] State Convention,* 17, 21; "Proceedings and Debates of the Mississippi State Convention of 1861. Reported by J. L. Power. First Session," 12, in John F. H. Claiborne Papers, Southern Historical Collection, University of North Carolina Library, Chapel Hill; *Jackson Weekly Mississippian,* Jan. 16, 1861.

23. *OR,* ser. 4, 1 : 42; William L. Barney, *The Secessionist Impulse: Alabama and Mississippi in 1860* (Princeton, N.J., 1974), 308–11; Lee, *Confederate Constitutions,* 14; Long, *Civil War Day by Day,* 23, 31.

24. For biographical data on Orr, see *DAB* 14 : 59–60; May and Faunt, *South Carolina Secedes,* 189–90; *Biographical Directory . . . American Congress,* 1373; Warner and Yearns, *Biographical Register . . . Confederate Congress,* 188–89; Roger P. Leemhuis, *James L. Orr and the Sectional Conflict* (Washington, D.C., 1979); Takaki, *Pro-Slavery Crusade,* 6, 107, 109, 185–92. See also James L. Orr to James Johnston Pettigrew, April 20, Oct. 30, 1857, Jan. 18, 1858, Pettigrew Family Papers, Southern Historical Collection, University of North Carolina Library, Chapel Hill.

25. *Keowee Courier* (Walhalla, S.C.), Dec. 1, 1860; Leemhuis, *Orr,* 73.

26. *Columbus Daily Enquirer,* Jan. 19, 1861; *Memphis Daily Appeal,* Jan. 22, 1861.

27. *Columbus Daily Enquirer,* Jan. 19, 1861; *Macon Daily Telegraph,* Jan. 18, 1861.

28. Michael P. Johnson, *Toward a Patriarchial Republic: The Secession of Georgia* (Baton Rouge, La., 1977), 113–17; Ulrich B. Phillips, *Georgia and State Rights* (rept. Yellow Springs, Ohio, 1968), 202–5; Long, *Civil War Day by Day,* 27–28, 31; Lee, *Confederate Constitutions,* 18.

29. For biographical data on Manning, see May and Faunt, *South Carolina Secedes,* 177; Myers, *Children of Pride,* 1616; Ralph A. Wooster, *The Secession Conventions of the South* (Princeton, N.J., 1962), 18–20.

30. *New Orleans Bee,* Jan. 26, 1861; *New Orleans Daily True Delta,* Jan. 26, 1861; *New Orleans Daily Picayune,* Jan. 26, 29, 1861.

31. *Official Journal of the Proceedings of the Convention of the State of Louisiana* (New Orleans, 1861), 17–18; Long, *Civil War Day by Day,* 29, 31; Lee, *Confederate Constitutions,* 18–19.

32. For biographical data on McQueen, see *Biographical Directory . . . American Congress,* 1277; Warner and Yearns, *Biographical Register . . . Confederate Congress,* 162–63; *Jackson Semi-Weekly Mississippian,* Dec. 21, 1860; White, *Robert Barnwell Rhett,* 184.

33. *Charleston Mercury,* Dec. 22, 24, 1860; *Charleston Daily Courier,* Dec. 25, 1860.

34. *Charleston Daily Courier,* Dec. 29, 1860.

35. Ibid., Feb. 19, 1861; Winkler, *Journal of the Secession Convention . . . Texas, 1861,* 50–52.

36. Walter L. Buenger, *Secession and the Union in Texas* (Austin, Tex., 1984), 148, 151–53; Long, *Civil War Day by Day,* 31, 36.

37. *Journal of the Convention . . . South Carolina . . . 1860, 1861, and 1862,* 277–78.

4. The Alabamians

1. S. F. Hale to L. C. Clark, Dec. 25, 1860, in C. C. Jones Jr., comp., Autograph Letters and Portraits of the Signers of the Constitution of the Confederate States, scrapbook in C. C. Jones Jr. Papers, Duke University Library, Durham, N.C. See also *Montgomery Weekly Mail,* Dec. 24, 1860.

2. *Montgomery Weekly Mail,* Dec. 14, 1860.

3. *Montgomery Weekly Post,* Dec. 19, 1860; *Montgomery Daily Mail,* Dec. 20, 1860; Smith, *History and Debates . . . Alabama,* 35.

4. For biographical data on Hale, see Brewer, *Alabama,* 266–67; Garrett, *Reminiscences of Public Men,* 665; Owen, *History of Alabama* 3 : 724–25; Warner and Yearns, *Biographical Register . . . Confederate Congress,* 108; Lee, *Confederate Constitutions,* 156; Thornton, *Politics and Power in a Slave Society,* 434.

5. *OR,* ser. 4, 1 : 4–15. For references to Hamlin's ancestry, see *Montgomery Weekly Mail,* Nov. 9, 1860, and *Charleston Mercury,* Jan. 22, 1861.

6. Dumond, *Secession Movement,* 223–25.

7. For biographical data on Curry, see *DAB* 4:605–6; *Biographical Directory . . . American Congress,* 870; Brewer, *Alabama,* 541–42; Owen, *History of Alabama* 3:444–45; Warner and Yearns, *Biographical Register . . . Confederate Congress,* 67–69; Lee, *Confederate Constitutions,* 156; Jessie P. Rice, *J. L. M. Curry: Southerner, Statesman, and Educator* (New York, 1949), esp. 22–36.

8. *OR,* ser. 4, 1:38–42.

9. *Montgomery Weekly Advertiser,* Dec. 12, 1860; J. L. M. Curry, "The Perils and Duty of the South, . . . Speech Delivered in Talladega, Alabama, November 26, 1860," in Wakelyn, *Southern Pamphlets on Secession,* 42, 45.

10. *St. Louis Daily Missouri Democrat,* Jan. 1, 1861. For biographical data on Cooper, see Brewer, *Alabama,* 189–90; Garrett, *Reminiscences of Public Men,* 489; *Northern Alabama, Historical and Biographical* (Birmingham, Ala., 1888), 432; Owen, *History of Alabama* 3:398–99.

11. Smith, *History and Debates . . . Alabama,* 437–43. For biographical data on Clopton, see *DAB* 4:230; Warner and Yearns, *Biographical Register . . . Confederate Congress,* 54–55; *Biographical Directory . . . American Congress,* 825; Brewer, *Alabama,* 481–82; Garrett, *Reminiscences of Public Men,* 730–31; *Northern Alabama,* 613–14; *Memorial Record of Alabama,* 2 vols. (Madison, Wis., 1893), 2:644–49; Owen, *History of Alabama* 3:352, 355; Marie B. Owen, *The Story of Alabama: A History of the State,* 5 vols. (New York, 1949), 2:319–21.

12. *OR,* ser. 4, 1:16. For biographical data on Shorter, see *DAB* 17:129–30; Warner and Yearns, *Biographical Register . . . Confederate Congress,* 219; Brewer, *Alabama,* 126–27; Owen, *Story of Alabama* 1:258–59; Owen, *History of Alabama* 4:1552, 1555; Garrett, *Reminiscences of Public Men,* 722–23; Lee, *Confederate Constitutions,* 156.

13. *OR,* ser. 4, 1:71–72. For biographical data on Calhoun, see Brewer, *Alabama,* 218; Garrett, *Reminiscences of Public Men,* 288–89; Owen, *History of Alabama* 3:285–86; Moore, *History of Alabama* 1:481.

14. *Richmond Daily Enquirer,* Jan. 21, 1861. For biographical data on Hopkins, see *DAB* 9:206–7; Brewer, *Alabama,* 403–4; Garrett, *Reminiscences*

of Public Men, 377–80; Owen, *History of Alabama* 3 : 843 –44; Owen, *Story of Alabama* 2 : 328–30.

5. The Mission to Virginia

1. Henry T. Shanks, *The Secession Movement in Virginia, 1847–1861* (Richmond, 1934), 148–50.

2. Ibid., 148–57; Wooster, *Secession Conventions,* 141–42. The best study of Virginia politics during the secession crisis is Crofts, *Reluctant Confederates.*

3. George H. Reese, ed., *Proceedings of the Virginia State Convention of 1861,* 4 vols. (Richmond, 1965), 1 : 18–19; *New York Times,* Feb. 15, 1861.

4. J. B. Dorman to James D. Davidson, Feb. 14, 1861, James D. Davidson Papers, McCormick Collection, State Historical Society of Wisconsin, Madison; William H. Gaines Jr., ed., *Biographical Register of Members, Virginia State Convention of 1861, First Session* (Richmond, 1969), 31–32.

5. Reese, *Proceedings . . . Virginia State Convention* 1 : 23; *New York Herald,* Feb. 16, 1861.

6. John S. Preston to [Francis W. Pickens], Feb. 17, 1861, John Smith Preston Papers, South Caroliniana Library, University of South Carolina, Columbia.

7. Reese, *Proceedings . . . Virginia State Convention* 1 : 23, 50.

8. Powhatan Ellis to G. W. Munford, Feb. 9, 1861, Misc. Letters and Papers, Virginia Executive Papers, Governor John Letcher, Library of Virginia, Richmond.

9. For biographical data on Anderson, see Lynch, *Bench and Bar of Mississippi,* 429–44; Rowland, *Mississippi . . . Sketches* 1 : 116; Percy L. Rainwater, *Mississippi, Storm Center of Secession, 1856–1861* (Baton Rouge, La., 1938), 193; *Vicksburg Daily Whig,* Dec. 12, 1860.

10. Entry for Feb. 18, 1861, John C. Rutherfoord Diary, Rutherfoord Family Papers, Virginia Historical Society, Richmond.

11. Reese, *Proceedings . . . Virginia State Convention* 1 : 50–62. The commissioners' addresses are available in two versions: a verbatim transcription taken down by stenographers in the convention hall as the speeches were

being delivered and a slightly different text published in pamphlet form later in 1861 by Wyatt M. Elliott, a Richmond printer. The verbatim transcripts as published in the *Richmond Enquirer* in 1861 form the basis for Reese, *Proceedings . . . Virginia State Convention,* and I have used this version unless the transcription is incomplete or is obviously garbled. In these instances, which are relatively rare, I have used the language in the pamphlet version: *Addresses Delivered before the Virginia State Convention by Hon. Fulton Anderson, Commissioner from Mississippi, Hon. Henry L. Benning, Commissioner from Georgia, and Hon. John S. Preston, Commissioner from South Carolina, February 1861.* Anderson's speech can be found on pp. 5–19 of this pamphlet.

12. *Richmond Enquirer,* Feb. 19, 1861.

13. For biographical data on Benning, see James C. Cobb, "The Making of a Secessionist: Henry L. Benning and the Coming of the Civil War," *Georgia Historical Quarterly* 60 (1976): 313–23; *DAB* 2:202–4; Kenneth Coleman and Charles S. Gurr, *Dictionary of Georgia Biography,* 2 vols. (Athens, Ga., 1983), 1:71–72; William J. Northern, ed., *Men of Mark in Georgia,* 7 vols. (Atlanta, 1907–12), 3:259–67; 56 *Georgia Reports* 694–99; Ezra J. Warner, *Generals in Gray: Lives of the Confederate Commanders* (Baton Rouge, La., 1959), 25–26.

14. Reese, *Proceedings . . . Virginia State Convention* 1:62–66.

15. Northern, *Men of Mark* 3:265–66.

16. Reese, *Proceedings . . . Virginia State Convention* 1:66–75; *Addresses Delivered . . . Virginia State Convention,* 42.

17. Reese, *Proceedings . . . Virginia State Convention* 1:75–76.

18. Robert Y. Conrad to Elizabeth Conrad, Feb. 18, 1861, Robert Y. Conrad Papers, Virginia Historical Society, Richmond. See also Gaines, *Biographical Register . . . Virginia State Convention,* 28–29, and David F. Riggs, "Robert Young Conrad and the Ordeal of Secession," *Virginia Magazine of History and Biography* 86 (1978): 259–60.

19. John Janney to Alice S. Janney, Feb. 18, 1861, John Janney Papers, University of Virginia Library, Charlottesville. See also Gaines, *Biographical Register . . . Virginia State Convention,* 49.

20. For biographical data on Preston, see *DAB* 15:202–3; May and Faunt, *South Carolina Secedes,* 195–96; Myers, *Children of Pride,* 1649; Warner, *Generals in Gray,* 245–46; *New York Times,* Nov. 28, 1860.

21. *Columbia South Carolinian,* quoted in *Montgomery Weekly Post,* Feb. 6, 1861.

22. Entry for Feb. 19, 1861, John C. Rutherfoord Diary, Rutherfoord Family Papers.

23. Reese, *Proceedings . . . Virginia State Convention* 1:76–93; *Addresses Delivered . . . Virginia State Convention,* 54, 56–57, 62.

24. Entry for Feb. 19, 1861, John C. Rutherfoord Diary, Rutherfoord Family Papers.

25. L. E. Harvie to John S. Preston, March 6, 1861, Francis W. Pickens Papers, Duke University Library, Durham, N.C. See also Gaines, *Biographical Register . . . Virginia State Convention,* 43.

CONCLUSION: APOSTLES OF DISUNION, APOSTLES OF RACISM

1. May and Faunt, *South Carolina Secedes,* 196.

2. John S. Preston, *Address before the Washington and Jefferson Societies of the University of Virginia, June 30, 1868* (Lynchburg, Va., 1868), 11–12, 14, 25. A copy of this pamphlet can be found in the J. L. M. Curry Collection, Alabama Department of Archives and History, Montgomery.

3. J. L. M. Curry, *Civil History of the Government of the Confederate States, with Some Personal Reminiscences* (Richmond, 1901), 28–29. See also Curry, "Legal Justification of the South in Secession," in *Confederate Military History,* ed. Clement A. Evans, 12 vols. (Atlanta, 1899), 1:1–58.

4. *Nashville Union and American,* Jan. 10, 1861.

5. *Journal of the . . . Convention . . . of Georgia,* 357.

6. *Atlanta Southern Confederacy,* March 15, 1861.

7. *Nashville Union and American,* Jan. 10, 1861.

8. *Montgomery Weekly Mail,* Dec. 14, 1860.

9. *Address of Hon. Wm. L. Harris, before the Agricultural Association, Jackson, November 12, 1858* (Jackson, Miss., 1858), 4–5.

Afterword

1. Jonathan Alter, *The Promise: President Obama, Year One* (New York, 2010), 39.

2. Ibid., 111, 130, 263–64, 402, 408; Jonathan Alter, *The Center Holds: Obama and His Enemies* (New York, 2013), 18–31, 33–34, 38–43; *New York Times*, Feb. 17, 2016.

3. *New York Times*, June 19–20, 2015; Michael Eric Dyson, *The Black Presidency: Barack Obama and the Politics of Race in America* (Boston, 2016), 237–42.

4. *New York Times*, July 11, 2015.

5. Charles B. Dew, *The Making of a Racist: A Southerner Reflects on Family, History, and the Slave Trade* (Charlottesville, 2016).

6. Betts & Gregory, Auctioneers, price list and market report, Aug. 2, 1860, broadside in Chapin Library, Williams College, Williamstown, Mass.

7. See *Apostles of Disunion*, 114–15. The most powerful recent study linking slavery and the possible economic origins of the Civil War is James L. Huston, *Calculating the Value of the Union: Slavery, Property Rights, and the Economic Origins of the Civil War* (Chapel Hill, 2003).

8. See *Apostles of Disunion*, 35. The most detailed case for the importance of the slave trade issue in bringing on the Civil War is David L. Lightner, *Slavery and the Commerce Power: How the Struggle against the Interstate Slave Trade Led to the Civil War* (New Haven, 2006).

9. *Wilmington* (N.C.) *Journal*, Feb. 21, 1861. The section of the Confederate Constitution dealing with the African slave trade reads as follows: Article I, section 7. 1. "The importation of African negroes from any foreign country other than the slave-holding States of the United States, is hereby forbidden; and Congress are required to pass such laws as shall effectually prevent the same." See *OR*, ser. 4, I: 94.

10. Robert H. Smith, *An Address to the Citizens of Alabama, on the Constitution and Laws of the Confederate States of America* (Mobile, 1861), 19. The section of the Confederate Constitution dealing with the domestic slave trade actually reads as follows: Article I, section 7. 2. "The Congress shall also have power to

prohibit the introduction of slaves from any State not a member of this Confederacy." See *OR*, ser. 4, I: 94.

11. *OR*, ser. 4, I: 40–42.

12. *Speech of Hon. A. H. Handy, Commissioner to Maryland from the State of Mississippi, Delivered at Princess Anne, on the First Day of January, A.D. 1861* (Jackson, 1861), 8.

13. *Addresses Delivered before the Virginia State Convention by Hon. Fulton Anderson, Commissioner from Mississippi, Hon. Henry L. Benning, Commissioner from Georgia, and Hon. John S. Preston, Commissioner from South Carolina, February 1861* (Richmond, 1861), 46–47, 50–51.

14. Ibid., 10.

15. Ibid., 30, 40–42. Speaking in Jefferson City on Dec. 29, 1860, William Cooper, Alabama's commissioner to Missouri, also denied there would be any effort on the part of the Deep South to reinaugurate the African trade. He knew no one, not "a single individual who was in favor of re-opening it," and he dismissed as "a humbug" any "talk about the re-opening of the African trade." Using language strikingly similar to that subsequently employed by Benning, Cooper insisted that such a move would be disastrous: "It would cause the Southern States to be flooded with slaves and merged in an element of barbarism." See *St. Louis Sunday Morning Republican*, Dec. 30, 1860.

16. See Dew, *Making of a Racist*, 108, 109–10; www.measuringworth.com, accessed Feb. 20, 2016.

17. See Dew, *Making of a Racist*, 141–45.

18. For biographical data on Moore, see William H. Gaines Jr., *Biographical Register of Members, Virginia State Convention of 1861, First Session* (Richmond, 1969), 60; William G. Shade, *Democratizing the Old Dominion: Virginia and the Second American Party System, 1824–1861* (Charlottesville, 1996), 88, 197, 243, 266, 288, 298; Henry T. Shanks, *The Secession Movement in Virginia, 1847–1861* (Richmond, 1934), 57, 163–65; Daniel W. Crofts, *Reluctant Confederates: Upper South Unionists in the Secession Crisis* (Chapel Hill, 1989), 315–16.

19. S. McD. Moore to James D. Davidson, March 10, 29, April 6, 1861, James D. Davidson Papers, McCormick Collection, State Historical Society of Wisconsin, Madison. The bank mentioned by Moore in his April 6 letter was

the Traders Bank of the City of Richmond, chartered by the Virginia General Assembly in 1860; see *Acts of the General Assembly of the State of Virginia Passed in 1859–60* (Richmond, 1860), 15–16.

20. See *Apostles of Disunion,* 35.

21. For biographical data on Williamson, see Glenn R. Conrad, ed., *A Dictionary of Louisiana Biography,* 2 vols. (New Orleans, 1988), II: 852–53; David D. Plater, *The Butlers of Iberville Parish, Louisiana: Dunboyne Plantation in the 1800s* (Baton Rouge, 2015), 127–28, 131, 150–51; Charles B. Dew, "The Long Lost Returns: The Candidates and Their Totals in Louisiana's Secession Election," *Louisiana History* 10 (1969): 359.

22. See Walter Johnson, *River of Dark Dreams: Slavery and Empire in the Cotton Kingdom* (Cambridge, Mass., 2013); Sven Beckert, *Empire of Cotton: A Global History* (New York, 2014); Edward E. Baptist, *The Half Has Never Been Told: Slavery and the Making of American Capitalism* (New York, 2014); Calvin Schermerhorn, *The Business of Slavery and the Rise of American Capitalism, 1815–1860* (New Haven, 2015).

23. Ernest W. Winkler, ed., *Journal of the Secession Convention of Texas, 1861* (Austin, Tex., 1912), 120–23.

24. See *Apostles of Disunion,* 111.

25. Ibid., 120.

26. *Berkshire Eagle* (Pittsfield, Mass.), Feb. 10, 2016.

27. See *Apostles of Disunion,* 17.

28. *Richmond Times-Dispatch,* July 12, 2015.

Index